A RUSHING
MIGHTY
WIND

A RUSHING
MIGHTY
WIND

ANGUS BUCHAN

MONARCH
BOOKS

Oxford, UK & Grand Rapids, Michigan, USA

Published by Monarch Books
an imprint of
Lion Hudson plc
Wilkinson House, Jordan Hill Road,
Oxford OX2 8DR, England
Email: monarch@lionhudson.com
www.lionhudson.com/monarch

ISBN 978 0 85721 555 0

Originally published by Christian Art Publishers,
PO Box 1599, Vereeniging, 1930, RSA ·
This edition 2014

Acknowledgments
Unless otherwise indicated, all Scripture quotations are
taken from the *Holy Bible*, New King James Version.
Copyright © 1979, 1980, 1982 by Thomas Nelson, Inc. Used
by permission. All rights reserved.
Scripture quotations marked KJV are taken from the *Holy Bible*,
King James Version. Copyright © 1962 by The Zondervan
Corporation. Used by permission.
Scripture quotations are taken from The Message.
Copyright © by Eugene H. Peterson, 1993, 1994, 1995, 1996, 2000,
2001, 2002 by NavPress Publishing Group. Used by permission.

A catalogue record for this book is available from
the British Library

Printed and bound in the UK, May 2014, LH26

Dedication

For those men and women who wish to live more than just an average Christian life; who make themselves available to experiencing the majesty of our Lord Jesus Christ through the Holy Spirit.

> "I have come that they may have life, and that they may have it more abundantly."
>
> ~ John 10:10

**"Who can this be?
For He commands even the
winds and water, and they obey Him!"**

~ Luke 8:25 ~

Contents

The Miraculous Power of the Holy Spirit in Our Time

Revivals of the Past

The Very First Revival and Our Future

Acknowledgments

I want to thank the Lord Jesus Christ for my dear wife, Jill, who waits patiently for me to come home from my many tours and preaching appointments; but who is continually encouraging me about spiritual things. My daughter Jilly Hull, who has become such a tremendous source of strength to me in these last days.

To Ronel Bauer and Sanel Kleinbooi. To CUM, in particular Chris Johnsen and his staff. To Sua du Plessis who so inspires me, especially in the area of work ethics – what an example. To Emile Johnsen, who is busy educating me with regard to the cyberspace world.

To George Carpenter, my producer of our TV programs *Grassroots* and *Family Time*, who, with Emile Johnsen, compiled the DVD that captured the awakening that took place at the Dead Sea.

My daughter Robyn Maclean who has kept me straight with regard to the content and layout of this and all my other books, and who has patiently and lovingly typed out this manuscript. Thank you, Robs. To the rest of my family who have walked this long road with me in Revival: Andy, Rochelle, Kyla, Jaimee, Lindi, Kai, Dougal, Robyn, Jayke, Tyler, Fergie, Ashleigh, Josiah (Buckkies), Nathan, Greg, Jilly, Callum and Reuben Angus.

Foreword

The experience on the first night in En-Gedi at our Feast of Tabernacles celebration in 2012 will always remain unforgettable for us. For over thirty years now the International Christian Embassy has carried out the annual celebration of the Feast of Tabernacles.

The opening event of the feast always takes place in the Judean Desert at the shores of the Dead Sea. The night was exceptionally hot at 38°C. During the worship, sweat and dust were everywhere. The speaker for that first night was Angus Buchan. It was his second appearance at the Feast of Tabernacles.

Already the year before, Angus challenged us all with his passion for Revival and with greater expectation for the supernatural. His ministry has become a great inspiration not only to the thousands of pilgrims in Jerusalem but also to countless more people around the world. Angus is a gift of God to the body of Christ. He is a true apostle of faith that inspires a hunger for God in all who hear him.

Down in En-Gedi on 30 September 2012, Angus

mounted the stage and started to read the Word of God, from the second chapter of Acts:

> When the Day of Pentecost had fully come, they were all with one accord in one place. And suddenly there came a sound from heaven, as of a rushing mighty wind, and it filled the whole house where they were sitting. Then there appeared to them divided tongues, as of fire, and one sat upon each of them. And they were all filled with the Holy Spirit and began to speak with other tongues, as the Spirit gave them utterance (Acts 2:1–4).

Already as he read the Word a fresh breeze started blowing. As he closed the Bible the wind became so strong that eventually our security personnel asked that the stage be evacuated. Only Angus stayed on and preached.

Then something else happened: within minutes the wind was mingled with gentle yet refreshing drops of rain. This was a highly unusual occurrence in the Judean Desert. At the same time backstage, the overheated wires of the transmission truck for the TV broadcast caught fire. It was not big but it interrupted some of the live transmission. Everybody who was there understood that all this was supernatural. All around people went onto their knees.

This year's theme for the Feast of Tabernacles was "The Spirit of Grace and Supplication", taken from Zechariah 12:10:

> I will pour on the house of David and on the inhabitants of
> Jerusalem the Spirit of grace and supplication; then they will
> look on Me whom they pierced. Yes, they will mourn for Him
> as one mourns for his only son, and grieve for Him as one
> grieves for a firstborn.

This prophecy speaks about one of the greatest yet-to-be fulfilled prophecies for the Jewish people: the spiritual Revival and restoration of Israel. Many other prophets refer to this, such as the prophecies that are described in Ezekiel 36 and 37. We chose this theme as we recognized that it is Revival that is needed most for the troubled region of the Middle East.

Now all three manifestations – wind, fire, and rain – are frequently used in the Bible as symbols for the work of the Holy Spirit (see Isaiah 44:3–4; John 3:8; Acts 2:2). I truly believe from my heart that God gave us a powerful sign of affirmation to our feast theme, "The Spirit of Grace and Supplication". God was telling us that He indeed passionately desires to pour out His Spirit on all flesh, Jews and Gentiles alike.

From that first night on we received testimonies of God changing people's lives. Reconciliation took place and people were filled by His Spirit. It increased our faith for Revival!

The wind, rain, and fire caused a significant disturbance to the evening programme. We had to ask the people to stay back in their seats, but we could not hold them back. Angus later wrote that he had never experienced a meeting like that. Normally, he said, one needs to convince people to come forward for an altar call, but here he asked them to stay back, but people came forward in their masses. So the biggest sign for me that night was not the wind, the rain or the fire, but the people of God.

The storm could have easily caused chaos or even mass panic among the four and a half thousand people who had gathered. This did not happen; rather, they rushed forward to receive prayer even though the ushers and the preacher encouraged them to stay back. The chaotic weather turned into a powerful manifestation of a church hungry for God.

This we also witnessed in the remaining days of the conference as we had record crowds in our early morning prayer meetings. They lingered till late at night in the worship afterglow of each evening celebration. A hungry people was met by God, who wants to give His Spirit freely. God indeed visited us and we will be eternally thankful for Him. Our faith also became bolder to expect more from God!

As you read this book, I pray that the same will happen to you. God wants to impart a fresh hunger for His presence and for the supernatural move of His Spirit in our hearts.

In many places around the world the church has lost its hope. But there is an answer for the world today and that is Revival. Nobody and nothing can stop the work of the Holy Spirit.

A move of the Spirit might cause our human structures to shake and it surely will stretch and challenge us, but it can bring desperately needed transformation to our cities and nations. Therefore this book, which you now hold in your hands, is a much needed book. It will change your heart and through that God can transform entire nations.

Dr Jürgen Bühler
Executive Director
International Christian Embassy, Jerusalem

Preface

We had the wonderful privilege of holding a campaign at the City Temple in London in 2010. We spoke for eight nights straight.

It was held in the beautiful cathedral that the Reverend Dr Joseph Parker built. He was born in the year 1830 and went home to be with the Lord in 1902. He turned London upside down for Jesus, at the same time that Charles Haddon Spurgeon was preaching at the London Metropolitan Tabernacle.

These two men were instrumental in bringing Revival to the city of London in those days. Almost 150 years ago, Joseph Parker stated:

> If we, as the church, do not get back to spiritual visions, glimpses of heaven, and an awareness of a greater glory and life, we will lose our faith. Our altar will become nothing but cold, empty stone, never blessed with a visit from heaven.

The Miraculous Power of the
Holy Spirit in Our Time

ONE

En-Gedi: A Modern-Day Miracle

I want to record the significance of what took place on 30 September 2012, at En-Gedi, the Dead Sea, in Israel. I have had the privilege and honour of witnessing a modern-day miracle, almost in an identical manner to the events in the Upper Room in Jerusalem over two thousand years ago. This is recorded in Acts 2.

I really believe Father God wants me to set aside one day to document this account before I forget some of the incidents that took place that evening. It changed my life forever. It not only changed my life, but also impacted the lives of approximately four and a half thousand believers from every part of the world.

The whole objective of this book is to glorify our Lord Holy Spirit. He is the One who is known as the Comforter, the Helper, and the Friend who sticks closer than any brother. He is also known as the Advocate. In Greek He is called the *Parakletos*. I love Him so much.

I believe that this book will lead many others into the intimacy of the knowledge of the living God, who dwells amongst us on this earth.

In John 16:7, the Lord said that it is imperative, it is expedient (profitable and in our favour) that He leave and return to His Father so that He could send the Helper. Jesus explained to His disciples that if He did not return to heaven, the Holy Spirit could not come. He, the Helper, would be with us always.

The beauty of having the Holy Spirit with me, and with you too, is that He can be everywhere at one time. Jesus could only be at one place at one time because He was made of flesh. The Holy Spirit can hover and move wherever He chooses, like a "mighty rushing wind".

I have asked God to forgive me for neglecting my relationship with my Lord Holy Spirit. But today that has changed. I have fallen in love once again with my Lord Holy Spirit, and with God. I asked a friend whether it is possible to be born again, again. If it is, then that is what has happened to me. My whole relationship with God has been turned around and made new. I have found a new dimension and experience with the living God. He is so tangible and so physically real to me.

Let me start my journey at the beginning. I was invited by the Christian Embassy to the Feast of Tabernacles for believers, which is held every year in September at En-Gedi.

The climax of the event takes place at the Dead Sea. The Feast of Tabernacles is one of the holy feasts that the Jewish nation remembers every year. It takes place over seven days and is a public holiday for the whole nation.

Time is taken to commemorate, to remember, and to honour God for the forty years they walked through the desert from Egypt to the Red Sea. Up through the merciless Negev Desert, up to the Jordan and then into the Promised Land they went. This in itself was miraculous, especially when one sees the treacherous country they had to walk through. There was no water to speak of, temperatures reaching up to 50°C, with minimal grazing for their animals. If we read the book of Exodus again, we will see that we serve a miracle-working God, beyond any shadow of a doubt.

As a farmer, as a man of the land, and as a naturalist, I can see it is physically impossible for a complete nation of approximately two and a half million people, along with all their worldly possessions – their sheep, cattle, goats, camels – to complete that journey. The Israelites were a decimated people, they were unregimented, and they had no structure because they had been slaves for so long. They had a "survival mentality" in which they literally lived from hand to mouth. They had been told what to do, when to do it, and how to do it. It was an absolute miracle that God could look after these people, in summer temperatures of up to 50°C. Their sandals never wore out, they continued in their day to day living, bearing children and raising families. God fed them every single day with manna from heaven. The Lord preserved the Jews for forty years, which the Bible often refers to as a generation. Every year, the Israelites commemorate the mighty God who took care of each one of them.

I had been invited as the keynote speaker at the Feast of Tabernacles. Just before I departed from South Africa to fly to Israel, the Christian Embassy contacted my office and requested the topic of my sermon along with a basic outline of the content. They wanted to prepare their interpreters for my message. Just about every nation under heaven sends delegates as representatives to En-Gedi for the feast. I asked the Lord for guidance and I felt the Lord wanted me to speak about Revival. John Wesley's definition of the word *revival* is "a people saturated with God".

We left OR Tambo International Airport destined for Tel Aviv on 28 September. Clive Tedder, a spiritual son, accompanied me. He was so excited and was expecting something to happen in his own life. He had no idea what was going to take place, and neither did I. Nobody did, for that matter. I could just imagine the delegates preparing themselves for a trip to the Holy Land, full of excitement and expectation. People from all over the world, every class, every creed, every tongue, were packing their suitcases – some had saved for years to go to the Promised Land (or "Jesus Country", as I like to call it).

At OR Tambo Airport, we met up with other pilgrims lined up at the El-Al ticket counter, waiting patiently to

> There was a great air of expectancy and excitement amongst the pilgrims.

check in. El-Al is regarded as the safest airline in the world because of their strict security systems. However, this does sometimes result in long queues of folk waiting patiently before being attended to. Security scrutinize every detail of luggage; they ask travellers many questions in order to prevent a passenger boarding who could harm the flight. There was a great air of expectancy and excitement amongst the pilgrims. People were chatting about what they planned to do once they landed in Israel. There was a real carnival atmosphere, photos were being taken, and laughter and excitement was everywhere.

Eventually, at about midnight, we started boarding the plane destined for Tel-Aviv International Airport. We had a safe flight and arrived early the following morning. We were met at the airport by lovely folk from the embassy and taken straight to our hotel. We washed, had a rest, and got ready for the event.

The last day of the month arrived – 30 September 2012 – a day that would change my life forever. We ate our meal, and as dusk was approaching, we were taken down to En-Gedi by a Swiss doctor. She had been working in Syria amongst the carnage taking place there. She drove us down to the event, held at En-Gedi down at the Dead Sea. It was an exciting trip. We left the most famous city in the world, Jerusalem, behind.

Jerusalem is built on the top of Mount Zion and it is the place where Solomon built the Temple. It is the place where Abraham offered up Isaac as a living sacrifice. It is the place our Lord Jesus entered for the last time while here on earth. Our emotions were running high.

We travelled down to the lowest point on earth, over 400 metres below sea level – a desert-like area. If you go south of the lake, you will go into the Negev Desert – the very place the Israelites would have walked up from when coming out of Egypt, to get to the modern-day Israel. It was known in those days as the land of Canaan – the land of milk and honey. The Israelites would have walked on the east side of the Jordan.

The Jordan River starts in Mount Hermon and flows downwards to the Sea of Galilee, also known as "Geneseret". From there it continues down and empties into the Dead Sea. Lake Galilee is shaped in the form of a harp; it is the most beautiful, the most fertile, and one of the most lovely fresh water lakes I have ever seen.

The lake teems with fish, even though it has been fished for thousands of years. The fish caught there is a type of Tilapia, a bream more commonly known as St Peter's fish. These are the very fish that were caught by the disciples and that the Master ate when He walked on this earth. All these physical realities really impact one when on a pilgrimage to the Holy Land. One's emotions become extremely sensitive and charged when one sits down and contemplates that this is actually the very place where God lived. This is the place where God came down from heaven to earth in human form. He actually could have eaten ate the same type of fish that I was eating.

This beautiful lake empties into the Jordan River, which flows down to the Dead Sea. The Dead Sea is completely opposite to the Sea of Galilee. It is the lowest point on earth; there is no life in it, not a living thing. The area is extremely hot, reaching up to 50°C in summer.

There is no wind or rain – in fact the landscape looks like the face of the moon: no grass, and no greenery except for a few groves of dates that are irrigated with water pumped from miles away. The Dead Sea has this name for a reason. Nothing can survive in its waters. The water is so full of minerals and salt that it is impossible for a man to drown in it. The water is so dense that one floats on the surface, the water itself keeping one buoyant. When we finally arrived at the Dead Sea, and opened the door of our air-conditioned vehicle, we were hit by a wave of intense heat. The smell of sulphur filled our nostrils, the same aroma encountered at an open cast mine.

En-Gedi is the place where David, Jesse's son, hid from Saul. Saul hunted David and tried to kill David because he felt threatened by the shepherd boy who was destined to become the king. There is a beautiful spring of fresh water that comes out of a steep cliff face and flows into the Dead Sea.

En-Gedi is a little oasis in an area of lifelessness, and is quite something to see. Surrounding the little spring and the flowing stream that cascades down the mountainside is life in abundance. Small antelope, dassies, birds, and plants flourish on the edges of the stream. That is where the life stops; the rest of the terrain is totally desolate. It is a rainless, windless, lifeless place.

TWO

A Wind of Change

I t took us an hour by road from Jerusalem to reach En-Gedi, set on the top of the mountain. We arrived at seven o'clock and the temperature was still over 35°C. We were each given a 1½ litre bottle of water and told to keep drinking!

We walked down to where the event was to be staged. There was a tremendous spirit of joy and celebration. There were people from just about every nation on the face of the earth. Folk were eating, the aroma of open fires and cooking meat hung in the air, and the sound of music filled the skies as the praise and worship team began the worship session. Not a breath of air was felt.

The stage had been erected near the edge of the lake. It was magnificent, with large side screens positioned on either side of the stage to enable people at the back to see clearly. I was impressed by the quality and standard of the setup.

Supper was over and a real carnival atmosphere had developed. People were happy, jovial, and there was the hum of a multitude of languages being spoken. Americans, Scandinavians, Europeans, Africans, and Asians – all were present. We were led to the front of the stage so that we would have easy access to the platform. People shook my hand and gave me hugs as I walked by, possibly recognizing me from the time I had spoken the year before. There was an amazing air of expectancy. I, too, felt expectant about what was going to happen. However, with the expectancy comes an awesome amount of pressure (obviously from the devil). I often feel this way before I speak. I feel totally inadequate and I have no idea what I'm going to tell the people.

I had been told that the keynote speaker from the year before was Renê Terra Nova. He is from Brazil and has a church of sixty-six thousand members. He oversees something like three million people. That is three times the total population of Swaziland! The year before that, the keynote speaker had been none other than Reinhard Bonnke. He is a dear friend and fellow "harvester", who has taken Africa for Jesus. Bonnke's favourite saying is: "Plundering hell and populating heaven for Jesus". He is definitely doing this on our beautiful continent of Africa. Bonnke has been known to speak to groups of a million people at a time.

You can imagine the pressure I was feeling; it was extreme, especially for a simple farmer. Yet I knew that the Holy Spirit was going to be with me, because He said He would be. When one takes one's eyes off the Lord, even for a moment, one starts to sink, just like Peter did on the Lake of Galilee: when he took his eyes off the Master, he too started to sink. So I became totally focused and I fixed my eyes on Jesus because I knew that without Him I was not going to accomplish anything.

A half hour before I was due to speak, the organizers called me aside to give me last-minute instructions as to what they wanted. I remember saying to the current president of the Christian Embassy, Dr Jürgen Bühler (a wonderful man of God, highly intelligent as a doctor of physics and an extremely humble man), "Jürgen, I want you to know that I will do nothing tonight without your permission; I am totally under your covering." His response was immediate: "We have been praying and fasting for this event for a long time; we are believing God for a *wind* of change," he said. I was also told by the director of the International Christian Embassy, a lovely man from Finland, that they had prayed that when Jürgen Bühler stood on the stage, the wind would blow so hard that his trousers would flap. None of us had any idea how prophetic those statements would be. Jürgen's trousers were almost blown off his body!

The praise and worship team was outstanding, a huge band, almost an orchestra, made up of musicians from

> We are believing God for a *wind* of change.

all over the world. There were violinists from Europe,

trumpeters from the USA, and singers from all parts of the world. They gave praise and honour to God.

The planning and organizing was magnificent. Dancers from all over the world performed, including a contingent from a ballet school in Moscow. They were beautifully dressed in Israeli garb. While the music team was leading the worship and the dancers were performing there was hardly a breath of air. The organizers reminded us to continue drinking water – it was stiflingly hot and I could feel the perspiration pouring off me. And yet the atmosphere was beautiful.

I was called up to the pulpit and introduced. I opened my large red study Bible and started reading from the New King James Bible (this Bible is very special to me as it has travelled the world with me). I greeted the people, got on my knees, and humbled myself before God and His people and prayed the Scripture from Psalm 19:14: "Let the words of my mouth and the meditation of my heart be acceptable in Your sight, O Lord, my strength and my Redeemer." I stood up and asked the people to open their Bibles to Acts 2, reading from the first verse. That portion of my Bible has lots of notes in the margins and all the verses are highlighted. It is probably the most used chapter in my Bible. You will understand why in a moment.

I read Acts 2:1–5:

Now when the Day of Pentecost had fully come, they were all with one accord in one place.

That is verse 1, and I can tell you that there was a tremendous unity and love at En-Gedi amongst the people of all nations, all denominations and all races – all praising the Lord.

> And suddenly there came a sound from heaven, as of a rushing mighty wind, and it filled the whole house where they were sitting. Then there appeared to them divided tongues, as of fire, and one sat upon each of them. And they were all filled with the Holy Spirit and began to speak with other tongues as the Spirit gave them utterance. And there were dwelling in Jerusalem Jews, devout men, from every nation under Heaven.

Then I asked the people to continue, reading verses 16 to 21:

> But this is what was spoken by the prophet Joel [hundreds of years before Pentecost]: "And it shall come to pass in the last days, says God, that I will pour out My Spirit on all flesh; your sons and your daughters shall prophesy, your young men shall see visions, your old men shall dream dreams. And on My menservants and on My maidservants I will pour out My Spirit in those days; and they shall prophesy. I will show wonders in heaven above and signs in the earth beneath; blood and fire and vapor of smoke. The sun shall be turned into darkness, and the moon into blood, before the coming of the great and awesome day of the Lord. And it shall come to pass that whoever calls upon the name of the Lord shall be saved.

Then I asked the people to read verse 41: "Then those who gladly received his word were baptized; and that day about three thousand souls were added to them."

I closed my Bible and I walked around to the front of the pulpit and started to preach. I said, "We are expecting a visitation from God's Holy Spirit here in Jesus Country. We are expecting a rushing mighty wind; we are expecting signs and wonders."

I went on to explain that this is not foreign to me, that I had seen God work in miracle-working power – blind eyes opened, deaf ears unstopped, the sick healed and the lame walk. I reminded the precious folk that our God is the weatherman; He controls the weather. I said, "I have seen Him bring rain where there was not supposed to be rain. I have seen Him grow crops out of dry ground." I went into detail about the miracle-working power of God; I said that people were praying for us all around the world, for a visitation of the Holy Spirit.

With that, the wind started to pick up. I need to stress that it is uncommon for that area to experience wind. A very trusted and reputable tour guide, Mushi (Moses), told me categorically that he had been bringing tour groups to En-Gedi for thirty-one years and he had never

> As I was praying it started to rain. The people started shouting and rejoicing.

encountered any wind to speak of, and there had never been rain!

The wind started quite gently, through the palm trees planted around the area. It started to intensify and

I asked the Holy Spirit to please come and fill us, and to let the wind of Revival blow into our lives.

I had been praying aloud when something quite amazing happened. As I was praying it started to rain. The people started shouting and rejoicing.

The wind then became quite ferocious. (I have since researched the rushing mighty wind in different Bible translations and these are some of the descriptions: "a rushing mighty wind", "a violent wind", and "a gale force wind" – all these different interpretations describe exactly what we experienced.)

I am a farmer and I study the weather. I have grown crops for forty years and so weather patterns are very important to me. A farmer needs to know when to plant crops, when to fertilize them, and when to harvest them. These are all dependent on the elements. This wind was not something I had ever seen before.

As I was preaching, the wind intensified. All of a sudden, I lost my Bible. My Bible weighs about 2 kilograms (5 pounds) and it blew off the platform like a piece of tissue paper.

> All of a sudden,
> I lost my Bible ...
> it blew off the
> platform like a piece
> of tissue paper.

The music stands started to collapse and the band members came running onto the stage to try to rescue the musical instruments and equipment. I looked around and found myself standing alone with a hand-held microphone. That evening I went through about three microphones.

Eventually I was given a microphone with a lead attached to it. It had no sponge covering the mouthpiece to muffle interference. This was significant because I record up to eleven episodes for my television programmes in one week. My producer, George Carpenter, is paranoid about interference and noise when we are recording outdoors. In fact, if there is the slightest breeze, he will stop recording and put the lapel microphone inside my shirt and make me turn my back to the prevailing breeze to avoid any possible sound interference. This was an absolute tornado I was preaching in, and when I watched the footage later I noticed that my voice came through clearly on the unprotected microphone – another miracle from God.

If you look a bit further on in Acts 2, you will see that after the baptism of the Holy Spirit, the disciples began to speak in different languages. People mocked them and some said that they were drunk. Peter reminded them that it was only nine o'clock in the morning, so how could they be drunk? The point I am trying to make is that whenever a miracle takes place, some people will always try to explain it away. It is sad to admit that some people cannot believe that Jesus still performs miracles on a daily basis, big ones and small ones. The greatest sin in the Bible is not murder or adultery or even theft; it is unbelief. Jesus can do nothing for us, if we choose not to believe.

The only time that our Master got angry with His disciples, as recorded in the New Testament, was when they would not believe Him. They doubted Him –

remember the incident with the young boy who was demon-possessed? Jesus said, "You wicked, perverse generation, bring him to Me." Jesus cast out the demon immediately.

If there is one prayer that I pray now, it is to ask the Lord Jesus to increase our faith and to believe for the impossible. As we know, faith is "the substance of things hoped for, the evidence of things not seen" (Hebrews 11:1).

Chapter

THREE

A Free-Spirited Revival

I love St Augustine's definition of faith: "Faith is to believe what you cannot see and the reward of that faith is to see what you believe."

That is exactly what happened to us at En-Gedi. The wind was so intense that the big side screens were ripped away. The whole steel structure of the stage started to shake. The designated Israeli stage crew started to panic. They tried to tie down the structure with ropes to prevent it from falling over. People were becoming uneasy and some a little fearful as the rushing mighty wind continued to intensify.

I asked the people to please sit down; I actually asked them to kneel down and pray, myself included. We prayed a prayer of repentance and asked God to forgive us of any sin in our lives. We asked God to fill us afresh with the Holy Spirit. We were literally filled afresh with

God's Spirit, and elation and an unexplainable joy filled us. People were singing, some were crying, and others were laughing.

I asked the Lord Holy Spirit to baptize all of us with His power – and people started to speak in their new languages that God had given them. It was amazing; it was like hearing voices from heaven. I, myself, felt such boldness, such liberty; there was no effort, no struggle, no embarrassment, no shyness, and no doubt. People were caught up in the tangible presence of Almighty God.

The wind began blowing even harder, and I asked the people to join me in singing praises to our God in our new language. My assistant, Clive, said he had never heard me sing like that before. He said it sounded operatic – and so it seemed to me, too. I love praising God and I love to sing, but I have never had professional tuition. As I sang my heart out for the Lord, I felt such freedom. After having sung in tongues for some time, the people, spontaneously led by the Spirit of God, started running to the front of the platform. They were not walking; they were running, hundreds of them. It was Holy Ghost chaos! I had spoken in my introduction of either a Revival or a riot. In this case it was definitely a Revival, a beautiful uncontrolled free-spirited Revival, and yet there was order.

> It was definitely a Revival, a beautiful uncontrolled free-spirited Revival, and yet there was order.

The pilgrims came to the front; they were kneeling, they were standing, and they had their hands raised to heaven in an attitude of complete surrender. The stage crew were running around and shouting at me to tell the people to get back from the stage because it was going to collapse. I say this with a smile, because I have never in my life asked a person to go back when they desire to make a public confession of their faith in Jesus Christ. They would not have listened to me anyway. We were truly drunk in the Spirit by this time.

The service continued, the wind blew, and I firmly believe that God did a sovereign work in people's lives that night. Sins were forgiven, sicknesses were healed, inferiority complexes were broken, and unforgiveness was dealt with once and for all. There was such elation, such joy.

After the service finally ended, the ushers tried to escort me to the vehicle, but people were pushing into me from all sides.

People were running up and trying to touch me. I felt quite scared because there is one thing I never want to do and that is to touch God's glory. What was quickened to my spirit at that time was the portion of Scripture after Jesus had been resurrected from the dead. Jesus said to Peter and John that it was expedient for Him to return to His Father in heaven so that He could send His Holy Spirit to abide with us as our Helper. When that happened, Peter and John laid their hands on the sick and they recovered instantly – because they were so filled with the power of God.

The Bible says that the people were laying the sick out in the street so that when the disciples passed by and their shadows fell on the sick, they were instantly healed. The pilgrims at En-Gedi were asking me to touch them; it was such a great honour to be recognized as one of God's humble servants. We eventually got back to the vehicle and returned to Jerusalem.

That night, I struggled to get to sleep. I have an iPad® with lovely worship music on it and I usually take a set of earphones with me when I travel. I turned on the music and allowed the gentle worship music to minister to my soul.

The band Jesus Culture was playing; the band leader was encouraging listeners to sing to the Lord in our heavenly language (another coincidence). I was caught up into the wonderful presence of God for many hours, eventually falling into a deep sleep.

> It had been an amazing encounter with God.

The next morning we went down to breakfast. There were quite a few delegates staying at the same hotel as I. We all ate together in a large dining room. Well, we hardly had a chance to eat anything! Clive, my assistant, said to me, "Please, Uncle Angus, let's try to have something to eat." I didn't get a chance. The delegates were greeting me, shaking my hand, hugging me, and taking photos with me. A miracle had taken place the night before and they had experienced it too. It had been an amazing encounter with God.

There had been a Norwegian film crew among the delegates at the meeting the previous evening. They had arrived from Scandinavia with a huge truck that they had shipped across to film the event – something they do annually. They are the only Christian TV channel in the whole of Norway.

Jan, who looks like a modern-day Viking, was a huge man with a beautiful laugh and smile and he asked me, "When are you coming to Norway, because we want the Viking spirit back again?" I trust we will get there one day. Jan had been standing next to his truck the night before, and, like the rest of us, stood in awe of what the Holy Spirit was doing.

A young Japanese man came running up to him, shouting, "Fire, fire!" The big Viking responded, "Ja, ja! It's the Holy Spirit."

"No, no. Fire!" shouted the young man again, pointing to Jan's truck. Jan turned around to find that his truck had actually caught alight.

I laugh when I think back on this experience and yet I stand amazed. Don't ever be concerned about storms in your life. Don't worry when things don't go according to the script. Our Lord Holy Spirit is too large, too massive, and too beautiful to be constrained by man. God will never be confined by man. There is a beautiful Scripture in Romans 8:28: "And we know that all things work together for good to those that love God, to those who are called according to His purpose."

I know, as a farmer, if there is no storm there can be no rain. There was once a storm I will never forget.

After the wind and the rain, people's lives were changed irrevocably and forever. At Shalom we hold to the saying: "One genuine miracle equals a thousand sermons." The miracle that four and a half thousand pilgrims witnessed spoke volumes to each one of us. No one will ever be able to convince me that there is no Holy Spirit, or that the experience at En-Gedi was just a figment of my imagination. It was just like John wrote in 1 John 1:2 (KJV): "For the life was manifested, and we have seen it, and bear witness, and shew unto you that eternal life, which was with the Father, and was manifested unto us."

John was talking about our Blessed Saviour, Jesus Christ. We, too, can give a testimony of having a physical encounter with our Lord Holy Spirit.

FOUR

Testimonies

The main objective of receiving the Holy Spirit is to enable us to be effective in the work Father God has chosen us to do. When God sends a man into battle, He does not send him in defenceless – and what is the point of going into battle with a pop gun, when God has a scud missile available for us?

Many of us refuse to take the weapons God has given us, often out of pride, and we end up as casualties of war. Without the Holy Spirit in our lives, we won't last.

As Joseph Parker said, we need the supernatural, we need vision, and we need the reality of Jesus Christ in order to keep our faith alive. Otherwise all we are, are sophisticated history teachers. People are sick and tired of instruction and school lessons – they want to see Jesus in reality; they want to experience the Lord for themselves. How can we convey a living

God to a lost world if we have never experienced Him ourselves?

The Bible says of the Upper Room experience, that *all* were filled with the Holy Spirit and received power from on high – not just a few privileged people. The Bible says in Matthew 7:7: "Ask, and it will be given to you; seek, and you will find; knock, and it will be opened to you." At the end of the day, we need to determine how desperate we are to meet with God.

"Those who wait on the Lord shall renew their strength; they shall mount up with wings like eagles, they shall run and not be weary, they shall walk and not faint" (Isaiah 40:31). That has become one of my favourite Scriptures in the Bible. Waiting can be so hard in this day and age because we are so programmed to be doing something all the time. If one goes to the shopping mall, it is so disturbing to see young people walking around with earphones in their ears listening to music, or sending text messages, totally oblivious to the people who are around them. We need to strike while the iron is hot. Jesus is not coming back soon – He is already on His way. The only way we will be able to win the lost is when the Master becomes a living reality to you and me.

> Jesus is not coming back soon – He is already on His way.

Many theologians are concerned *about* Jesus, instead of getting to know Jesus personally. Colossians 1:27 says, "Christ in you, the hope of glory." It is not about us; it is about the Lord living in our hearts – that is what will win souls to Christ quicker than anything else. When people see the love and passion in your heart for them, they will acknowledge Jesus as Saviour. There is one very important component of being a friend of Jesus and seeking the power of the Holy Spirit: He is not only the Spirit of God, He is also the Holy Spirit and will only dwell in a house that is clean and without sin.

We cannot serve two masters: we are either with Him or we are against Him – there is no in between. The greatest enemy we have in serving the Lord is not the devil, it is the self, the flesh. My biggest enemy is Angus Buchan. When Angus dies, then Jesus can live in him. Paul said in Galatians 2:20, "I have been crucified with Christ, it is no longer I who live, but Christ lives in me, and the life which I now live in the flesh I live by faith in the Son of God, who loved me and gave Himself for me."

There is an old Methodist hymn that says, "All of self and none of Thee", in the first verse, then "Some of self, and some of Thee", "Less of self, and more of Thee", and finally, "None of self, and all of Thee".

That is exactly how we must desire to live if we want to experience the manifestation of the living God through our lives. We need to die to the self; we need to live for Jesus and we need to live for our fellow man. The confirmation that we have of Jesus living in our hearts will be peace, joy, and, most of all, love.

I am personally experiencing that right now – I have an indescribable peace and joy that comes from having personal communion with the Holy Spirit. Seek Him while He may be found.

Clive Tedder assisted me during the trip to Israel. He too met tangibly with the Holy Spirit. Here is his written account:

We departed from Jerusalem on the Sunday afternoon at about 6 p.m. for the En-Gedi Desert where Uncle Angus was to be the keynote speaker for the Feast of Tabernacles in Israel. Once we had left the "New" Jerusalem, we travelled for a solid hour "downhill". The Dead Sea is approximately 415 metres below sea level, in the En-Gedi Desert where Uncle Angus was preaching.

On arrival the intense heat and stillness literally engulfed us as we climbed out of the air-conditioned vehicle. I have travelled a fair amount in Africa, but have never experienced heat like that... almost overbearing!

We made our way down to the stage, through an expectant, yet remarkably subdued, crowd of in the region of four and a half thousand people, from all the nations of the world. The praise and worship was truly special and coordinated only a few days before the event by teams from around the globe.

The weather was still incredibly hot and dead calm. Uncle Angus was introduced by Jürgen Bühler, head of ICEJ. Uncle Angus started preaching from Acts 2:1–4, the Upper Room experience. He claimed in faith that people would be changed that night, that people would speak in new tongues. He said we would see the Holy Spirit in a new way. He called the Holy Spirit down. It was not long after that that a "mighty rushing wind" came from nowhere!

My NIV Bible says in that Scripture that it was a "violent rushing wind". Well, that wind was almost violent! It appeared from nowhere and it was no normal wind. Speak to any geologist, a wind does not blow from the north, south, east, and west all in the space of twenty minutes... this did! I tell you it was the Holy Spirit moving in a way I have never seen. It was not tangible... it was physical! I saw the Holy Spirit move in the En-Gedi Desert, like a mighty rushing wind!

The stage equipment was pushed over, as the first gust came. A few of us tried to hold everything up; we resorted to laying it all flat on the ground. We thought it quite significant. Almost as if we had to lay everything aside so that the Lord could reveal Himself to us in a unique way! Flags of the different countries were also ripped out of people's hands and flew across the front of the stage. I went to collect Uncle Angus's thick leather-bound Bible that had been blown across the stage.

There was almost a danger of panic and fear coming across the people, but Uncle Angus, recognizing this as the Holy Spirit, kept people calm and continued to preach in his unique way. He called down the Holy Spirit even more and gave Him so much place to move and do His work that night.

During this time he said we wanted to see the Holy Spirit come down like fire... well a little later one of the technicians came running past us shouting "Fire, fire!"

A Norwegian TV producer responded, saying, "Ja, the fire of the Holy Spirit" – meanwhile his broadcasting lorry was on fire, due to the electrical cables being tossed around! Earlier in the hotel I prayed with Uncle Angus and asked for Holy Ghost chaos... phew, I never thought God would answer my prayer so dramatically! The evening concluded by Uncle Angus leading people to pray in tongues. For many, it was their first time! This was followed by many singing in tongues, so sweetly; one could hear it was from the Holy Spirit!

When the wind was at its strongest, the stage manager rushed us off, but Uncle Angus stayed on. I noticed the stage staff tightening the safety straps until they could no longer crank them anymore. Had the straps behind the stage snapped, that huge 6-metre-plus structure would have catapulted forward! Being concerned and responsible for his safety, I worked out it would've landed directly on Uncle Angus. So I edged forward, prepared to "rugby tackle" him off the stage! (In a way I was looking forward to that... I haven't put in a good tackle for a few years!)

On the way back to Jerusalem amid all the excitement I relayed this to Uncle Angus. His response was, "You needn't have worried; had the structure fallen on me it would've bounced off! God's presence was so real there, I think that would've happened. In fact, the structure should've come down; I think it was only God who kept it up."

When Uncle Angus was wrapping up, he called the lead singer to come and sing with him. The wind died down and we left, never to be the same again! Just as the disciples did after their Upper Room experience (see Acts 2:7–12), the people said, "We have never seen anything like it." In verse 37 the disciples said, "What do we do now?" Well, they preached the Gospel like never before; the power of the Holy Spirit was in them and worked through them mightily. We need to do the same!

The meeting ended (physically), but we all knew that spiritually this was a new beginning. The Holy Spirit had touched each of our hearts in such a significant way. Uncle Angus himself said that in all his years of preaching, he had never experienced a move of the Holy Spirit such as what happened that evening. He said he would never again preach without first acknowledging and giving the Holy Spirit place to move.

The Holy Spirit came that evening... in full force.

I received a letter from a lady called Marlene. It reads as follows:

Dear Angus,

In a book on Smith Wigglesworth, I came across the following extract of a manifestation of power experienced by the author in Norway, which mirrors your encounter at the Dead Sea. How God is moving mightily across the waters and setting the people alight with His flames of fire. Praise God.

The quotation comes from Stanley Frodsham's *Smith Wigglesworth: Apostle of Faith*:

The two policemen grabbed Wigglesworth and started pushing him through the crowd. He had arrived in Norway only that morning but word of him had spread before his arrival. Thousands surrounded the town hall hoping to get inside but unfortunately not another person could fit. Packed like sardines, the people inside were so tightly squeezed together no one could have tripped and fallen to the ground.

Having heard the rumours that a man who was able to perform miracles would be there, people had flocked to the hall from far and wide. Many were not Christians but they had come to witness and to seek the healings and other miraculous events that might happen.

With much difficulty, the policemen struggled to get Wigglesworth to the front of the hall. As he stood on the platform looking out over the vast crowd he was consumed with such tremendous zeal for the Lord and compassion for the people that he cried out, "God, give me a message that's different, that something might happen here that is different from anything else."

As Smith began to preach, the voice of God inwardly spoke to him: "If you will ask Me, I will give you every soul." Had he heard correctly? He continued to preach. "If you will ask Me, I will give you every soul." He struggled. He knew now it was the voice of the Lord, but he was slow to respond. Once again the message came: "If you believe and ask Me, I will give you every soul."

> From every direction a wind seemed to blow – the breath of the Holy Spirit.

Wigglesworth stopped. Every eye was upon him. Why had he stopped preaching? With his eyes closed he prayed, "All right, Lord, please do it. I ask You, please give me every soul."

From every direction a wind seemed to blow – the breath of the Holy Spirit swept over the auditorium from the front to the back. People all over the town hall began crying out to God for mercy. Every man, woman and child became acutely aware of personal sinfulness and unworthiness before this awesome God whom they were now experiencing. As they begged God's forgiveness, Wigglesworth pointed them to Jesus and the way of salvation.

With all of the yielding to Christ, God saved every soul just as He had spoken to this man who was "filled with God."

The following are messages I received since returning from En-Gedi:

I live in East London, South Africa. This morning the wind was really blowing and the Holy Spirit shared with me that "the Baruch", the Breath of God, gave Adam life and on the Day of Pentecost the disciples were anointed with the Holy Spirit. Fire that came as a rushing wind, the Baruch and God called Ezekiel in chapter 37 to summon the Baruch by prophecy to breathe life into the dead bones and likewise the Baruch manifested when Angus was ministering in En-Gedi in Israel at the Feast of Tabernacles, the last Feast that Jesus still has to fulfil, and God is raising up the dead bones of His people to get ready as the Bridegroom is soon to appear.

Robert

I was in the crowd. Every word you wrote about the experience at En-Gedi is true. Amen. Amen. Do you remember the pink flag or cloth that rose when the wind started to blow? God is great. We have been part of a visit of the Holy Spirit.

Johan

I was there and will testify to the accuracy of everything said about the night at En-Gedi. The only thing I will respectfully disagree with is the statement by some, "That we will never see anything like it again." No, we will see greater things! For our God never does the same thing twice. The next time

He wants to show up and show off for the world to see, it will be mightier.

Expect greater things from Him and we will receive greater things. Glory be to Yahweh and His Son, the Lord Yeshua (Jesus Christ) and His Holy Spirit forever – Amen!

Alan

The Holy Spirit moved in a wonderful way, and fell on us all.

André

It was a privilege and honour and being so blessed to be part of the Holy Ghost experience that you had together with my wife, Karen, and son André at En-Gedi down at the Dead Sea that evening. At the time when you came onto the stage my wife and I came forward and positioned ourselves right in front. All I can say is that it was an unbelievable experience that took place that evening, and confirms herewith the testimony you have made that the Holy Spirit was definitely present.

Pieter

I want to praise the Lord. Two or three weekends before the Israel tour we visited Shalom one Sunday morning and were fortunate to bump into you and managed to have a quick chat to you, during which you invited us to the opening of the Feast of Tabernacles, as this was not included in our Gospel Gala Tour.

Coincidently, we bumped into you again at the airport in Israel, when you reminded/invited us again to join you for the opening event on the Sunday night in the En-Gedi

Desert. We had managed to arrange this with our tour guide, not really knowing what this was all about or what to expect.

On arrival after a long hot, humid day, we settled into our seats in very warm conditions, and the compactness of the crowd did not help either with the humidity.

Before such an event I pray that God's presence might work in the mightiest of ways, I asked God to work mightily through the praise and worship and those who brought His message so that many lives may change/be revived! I went even further, which I by the way have never done before, for God to not speak to me in Morse code but to give me a sign (arrogant of me, I thought), and a slight breeze to make conditions a little more pleasant.

Before I could open my eyes I saw a flash in my right eye. Thinking it came from a camera, my wife advised me that it was lightning... to my great amazement.

There was a strong young man in front of me who was dressed in a white dress with some sort of cloth on his head, like the Muslims wear. In the beginning of the evening he had no interest in what was about to happen and advised me that he was only there as a translator for a lady of another country. He was more interested in talking to me about soccer and Bafana Bafana than in what was about to happen.

Once the Holy Spirit had moved in such a mighty way his cap was off and he was praying and worshiping much better! Afterwards he advised me with great excitement that he had never seen such a miracle – wind and rain in the desert! Praise the Lord!

Deon & Hester

Thank you for your blessing to Israel on Sunday night at En-Gedi. I was not there physically, but I was watching online live. What I saw (in faulty transmission due to the story) was the Holy Spirit being poured out with wind, fire and water (rain)!

The Lord, through you, blessed the whole ICEJ Feast, sanctioning it then and there as He flowed through you and your humble heart and life. I'll never forget seeing that blast of forceful wind telling us that God Himself by His Spirit was there! What a mighty God we serve. He is faithful! And you are tops! Thank you again for obeying God by coming to His home, Israel.

Linda

The next powerful testimony comes from an Orthodox Jew named Mushi (from the name Moses), whom I mentioned earlier. He is an extremely well-known and respected tour guide leader, and heads up a substantial tour business in Jerusalem. He has been bringing tour groups down to En-Gedi for the past thirty-one years. He had never encountered wind and rain like he saw at En-Gedi on the night of 30 September 2012. Out of the mouth of an Orthodox Jew came the confession that a huge miracle had taken place and we give God the praise for that.

> I'll never forget seeing that blast of forceful wind telling us that God Himself by His Spirit was there!

We continue with testimonies:

I was there! It was unbelievable and unforgettable! Our God is alive.

Ida

I was there, it was awesome! A modern-day miracle indeed! God is the same yesterday, today and tomorrow! Brother Angus, you are a blessed man of God. Amen!

Glenda

I was there; it was the most awesome experience of my life.

Maryke

I was there on my birthday, 30 September 2012, a life-changing experience!! Glory to God!

Alta

My husband and I were there... no words can describe the glory... thank You, God!

Carolynn

We were there, and it was amazing and awesome. What bewilderment.

Pieter

I just watched you here in SA on God TV. I was deeply moved. I watched the video of you at the Dead Sea, amazing!

Doug

FIVE

God Encounters

As I write this, I am sitting in a very quiet and desolate part of our farm. It is on the edge of a plateau looking out onto a large wetland. This is the source of the Umvoti River, which discharges some 60 kilometres away from here into the Indian Ocean. There are reeds in the wetland that stand almost 3 metres high in places, with large ponds of water. It is a bird sanctuary, one of the best I've seen. In the background I can hear a pair of Crested Cranes; it is the season for mating and they are pairing off.

My spirit is always moved when I see the Long-crested Eagle. I watched him soaring back and forth, oblivious to my presence, so close that I can almost see his eyes. The eagle was playing with the wind thermals; he was being swept high into the heavens, piercing the skies with his screams. Then he would swoop down low and glide along the edge of the plateau, hunting for small game or rabbits. He would catch another thermal that would take him high into the sky, where he would swoop down once again without needing to flap his wings. This is such a beautiful illustration of the power of the Holy Spirit, who comes like a rushing, mighty wind.

Our Lord Holy Spirit should be enjoyed by His creation. He should not be abused in any way but rather appreciated. We need not be afraid of the Holy Spirit, but should revere Him. Jesus sent the Holy Spirit to be with us constantly, twenty-four hours a day and seven days a week. He will never leave us and never forsake us (see Hebrews 13:5).

As I watched the magnificence and agility of this warrior of the sky, I felt elated and my spirit was quickened within me. I recalled the verse in Romans 8:11, "But if the Spirit of Him who raised Jesus from the dead dwells in you, He who raised Christ from the dead will also give life to your mortal bodies through His Spirit who dwells in you."

The Lord sent His Spirit for you and me, that we might live an abundant life. We need never feel afraid or lonely again; we need never feel incompetent or inadequate.

> The Lord sent His Spirit for you and me, that we might live an abundant life.

The Long-crested Eagle showed me the simplicity of the Holy Spirit, in a practical way. It is amazing how God speaks to us through the elements and through creation.

Maybe as farmers we listen better and are more observant when it comes to natural manifestations.

We have a pair of Burchell's Coucal in our garden – commonly known in Africa as the "rain bird". The call is definitely one of my favourites. He is not much to look at, but he has one of the most distinct calls. It is like a liquid, bubbling "doo-doo-doo-doo", descending in scale, then rising towards the end. This bird is the most reliable weather report that we have. When they start calling, best you get prepared, because rain is on its way. How does the coucal know that rain is coming? He must have a hotline to heaven.

The other day I was asked by a city boy, "How does one know from which direction a storm is approaching?" I answered, "Look at the direction in which the horse is facing. They will always stand with their backs to the oncoming storm." The principles of nature are always very simple and very straightforward. If we do not understand the principles, we do not see. Many times the

> If Jesus Christ sent His Holy Spirit to be our Guide and our Friend, why should we panic?

Lord has shown me the way He wants me to live – not exist, but *to live*. Often He has used creation to show me.

You will never find a "flock of eagles" flying together. An eagle is a solitary bird; he spends time in the high places. He is not like a crow or other scavengers that fly in groups and scrounge for all the left-overs. He flies high and he flies on his own or with his mate. He flies with a purpose.

The Long-crested Eagle that I was watching was enjoying life to the full. It looked like he hadn't a care in the world. That is how it should be with you and me. If Jesus Christ sent His Holy Spirit to be our Guide and our Friend, why should we panic?

Paul said in Philippians 1:21, "For to me, to live is Christ, and to die is gain." Therefore it is impossible to frighten a Spirit-filled believer, because if he lives he lives for God and if he dies he goes home to heaven to be with his loving Father forever.

As a young believer, I remember going to pray and fast for six days. I took clean, fresh water from the farm, a one-man tent that I pitched next to my pick-up, and my Bible. In those days there were no cell phones so I had contact with no one, not even my wife, Jill. I was at total peace because I knew Jesus would take care of my family while I was spending time with Him. The purpose of my retreat was to seek direction from God about the way forward. I went to a huge dam called Craigieburn; it was the middle of the week so I expected there to be fewer people at the dam, which would allow me complete peace to hear the voice of God.

I arrived to absolute peace and stillness; there was not another person in sight. After the third day I was extremely hungry. When I get hungry, I start to quieten down – and by nature I am not a quiet person! In fact Jill will tell you that I never stop talking.

They say that people who talk a lot, don't listen too well. That is why fasting is such a good practice for me to follow. After the third day of consuming only water, and plenty of it, my senses were extremely sharp. I was very observant, noticing things I would not normally see in the daily rat race of the life I live.

I could see more clearly, I could smell many of the fragrances of the wild flowers and trees, and I could hear more clearly. I went for a slow walk as it was very hot. I had a conversation with my Lord Holy Spirit and I asked Him, "Lord, why am I doing this?" It was as if the Lord answered me audibly. He said, "I'm going to show you how I want you to live."

Just then a flock of Spur-winged Geese circled the huge dam of a couple of kilometres in length, and landed in a bay. There were probably about twenty or thirty of these birds. They were totally unruly, squabbling and quaking and fighting with one another. Some birds were ducking under the water looking for fish, others were swimming around with their young, and the whole scene was chaotic. The Lord impressed on me that that is how the world is: people rushing here and there but not accomplishing much and not really getting anywhere.

I then felt the Holy Spirit tell me to lift up my eyes to the skies. I lifted up my head and I saw a small dot in the clear blue sky. I heard a shriek that only an African bird lover would recognize – it was the unmistakable call of the majestic African Fish Eagle.

Before I could see him, I could hear him. I recognized that small dot to be the fish eagle. I felt the Lord saying to me, "Watch him!" The eagle circled the big dam once, twice, then folded in his wings and dropped towards the water like a stone, straight as an arrow towards the water's surface. He flew down at a rate of knots, and as he was descending the Spur-winged Geese saw him and panicked. They did not know what to do. Some tried to dive under the water and others tried to take off. The diving eagle had his eye on a fish and just before he hit the water he locked his wings and glided on a wind thermal across the face of the water. He gave a shriek of utter contempt towards the geese and took off without even flapping his wings. The eagle then caught another thermal and disappeared into the sky.

After watching this whole episode, I felt the Lord say to me, "That is how I want you to be: I want you to come aside; I want you to be separate from this world. I have a specific work for you. Do not conform to the things of this world but be transformed by the renewing of your mind."

That was many years ago and yet I will never forget it. The Lord showed me so clearly that if I am to be used by Him then I must be prepared to completely separate myself from the things of this world. I need to remain unaffected by the fickleness of man and hear from God alone.

These unique "God encounters" can change a person's life forever. In the daily devotional *Streams in the Desert*, by Mrs Charles Cowman, I was reminded how the Father speaks clearly to us through these "Upper Room" experiences:

George Fox: I knew Jesus, and He was very precious to my soul; but I found something in me that would not keep sweet and patient and kind. I did what I could to keep it down, but it was there. I besought Jesus to do something for me, and, when I gave Him my will, He came to my heart, and took out all that would not be sweet, all that would not be kind, all that would not be patient, and then He shut the door.

Lady Huntington: My whole heart has not one single grain, this moment, of thirst after approbation. I feel alone with God; He fills the void; I have not one wish, one will, one desire, but in Him; He hath set my feet in a large room. I have wondered and stood amazed that God should make a conquest of all within me by love.

Bishop Hamline: All at once I felt as though a hand – not feeble, but omnipotent; not of wrath, but of love – was laid on my brow. I felt it not outwardly but inwardly. It seemed to press upon my whole being, and to diffuse all through me a holy, sin-consuming energy. As it passed downward, my heart as well as my head was conscious of the presence of this soul-cleansing energy, under the influence of which I fell to the floor, and in the joyful surprise of the moment, cried out in a loud voice. Still the hand of power wrought without and within; and wherever it moved, it seemed to leave the glorious influence of the Saviour's image. For a few minutes the deep ocean of God's love swallowed me up; all its waves and billows rolled over me.

Jonathan Edwards: Holiness – as I then wrote down some of my contemplations on it – appeared to me to be of a sweet, calm, pleasant, charming, serene nature, which brought an inexpressible purity, brightness, peacefulness, ravishment to the soul; in other words, that it made the soul like a field or garden of God, with all manner of pleasant fruits and flowers, all delightful and undisturbed, enjoying a sweet calm and the gentle vivifying beams of the sun.

We can be so easily sidetracked if we don't focus on God alone. I love what the old, blind Scottish preacher, George Matheson, said: "My goal is God Himself. I am seeking the Giver, and not the gift." To me that is so profound. If we expect a visitation from the Holy Spirit, we cannot be distracted by the things of this world.

> We can be so easily sidetracked if we don't focus on God alone.

A good example of this was the time my son Greg and I were being collected from OR Tambo International Airport. I had an appointment to speak in Pretoria. As we were driving towards the city with our host, Lukie, Greg said that he had read an article in the newspaper inferring that I had had something to do with the shooting of stray dogs on a farm in the Western Cape. The stray dogs had belonged to farm workers and had been shot in front of the children. Understandably, the children were traumatized. At the time of the alleged accusation against me, I was at the opposite end of the country – Jill and I were having a break, travelling around the Kruger National Park.

I discussed this false story with Lukie while we were travelling in the car. I asked Lukie what he would have done. His comment is one that I shall never forget. He said in perfect Latin, *"Aquila non captat muscas"* (the eagle does not hunt flies).

If we want to be used by God in these last days, we need to focus our energy on issues that have a kingdom value. We should not waste our time on matters that lead us down a cul-de-sac and have no real consequence to the things of God. Father God was telling me clearly through these illustrations of nature that I need to be spending more time with Him. I am obeying the Lord in this regard and have the privilege of spending up to five hours a day in His presence.

There have been times when God has spoken to me through the wind; and wind can be a life saver. When we first bought our farm, we had no money to spare. We didn't even have enough money to buy an electrical water pump to supply water to the house. We resorted instead to a windmill. We were completely dependent on the wind for our water supply. With five children in the house, we needed wind twenty-four hours a day. When the wind blew hard, the big water tank would overflow with beautiful clean, fresh water from a spring. But when there was no wind we had to look for water elsewhere. Our family quickly realized that wind was a necessity for life.

Wind can also be extremely destructive. I have encountered some devastating forest fires in my farming career. During the dry season, everything is bone dry.

Farmers are on standby, waiting for the dreaded mayday call that notifies the community of a fire outbreak. The wind can blow that fire into an inferno in a matter of minutes and these fires can be unstoppable.

A good farmer will learn how to manage the wind. An experienced farmer or forester will use the wind to his advantage when fighting a bush fire – by back burning. The farmer will start a fire on a firebreak and get the fire to burn backwards towards the oncoming runaway fire. In this way the fire will burn itself out. That's where the saying, "Fight fire with fire" comes from. An inexperienced farmer could lose everything he owns by not understanding the wind or the season.

In South Africa, autumn is the season when the farmer prepares his firebreaks. This protective measure ensures that if a fire breaks out in the dry season, he can fight it on neutral ground, as a base line has been established. The breaks are made by hoeing out the grass, or alternatively the area is sprayed in summer with a weed killer. Once the grass is dead, it is burnt – before the frost and fire season begin. There should be no flammable matter anywhere on the break area. If the breaks are not properly prepared and maintained, the fire will simply jump the break and destroy the forest or pasture land.

The moral of the story is that we need to do our homework. We need to understand the wind, just like a good sailor does; he knows how to trim his sails to get safely to his destination.

The Upper Room

As Christians, we need to understand the Holy Spirit and the sole purpose and reason for Him being sent to earth by Jesus. It is to help us – you and me – to finish this earthly pilgrimage. His very name implies His reason for being here. It is *Parakletos*, meaning "Helper".

It distresses me a great deal to hear of people who disregard the presence of the Holy Spirit. He is a gentleman. He is all-powerful, but He is also sensitive; He will not force Himself into anyone's life. He will not try to undermine the sovereignty of Jesus or our heavenly Father.

The Holy Spirit is regarded as a mirror; He reflects the glory of God. He will not try to take the place of Jesus; He is Jesus in the Spirit. This forms the Holy Trinity: Father, Son, and Holy Spirit. The three are one and yet they are different entities.

It comes back to raw faith at the end of the day. We could argue and discuss what we believe and do not believe. But I am not interested in your opinion, and you should not be interested in mine.

At the end of the day, it is only God's Holy Word that counts. When we read 1 John 5:7, we see that it is stated very clearly and simply that there are three who bear witness in Heaven: the Father, the Word, and the Holy Spirit. Who is the Word? His name is Jesus Christ, and so we take God's Holy Word literally as it is written. The Word was written by ordinary people, but they were all inspired by the Holy Spirit.

> There has never been a more well-read book or a book that has been treated with as much reverence as the Holy Bible.

The Bible has stood the test of time; it is still the best-seller of all the books that have ever been printed in the history of mankind. There has never been a more well-read book or a book that has been treated with as much reverence as the Holy Bible.

I remember, many years ago, visiting a Muslim. He invited us into his lovely home and asked us to be seated in his lounge. We sat down on beautiful chairs; I had my Bible in one hand. I was offered a cup of tea so I put my Bible down on the plush carpet next to my chair.

The Muslim jumped up from where he was seated to pick up my Bible, very reverently. He placed it on the table and said to me, "Please don't put that book on the floor!" He was right, and I have never done that again.

In fact, the Bible (God's Word in print) is so special to me that I cannot bring myself to place another book on top of it. This is not because I'm superstitious, but because I have developed a sincere respect for the Word.

A desperate young man once came to see me after a campaign meeting I was holding. He was weeping. He was a very good-looking young man, a civil engineer by profession who held a senior position despite being in his mid-twenties. He was in a terrible state. I had been speaking about the simplicity of the gospel and of believing the Holy Spirit.

He said to me, "I am so confused. I can't settle down to think rationally. It has got so bad that my girlfriend has broken up with me; she can't understand where I am coming from. There are so many questions at work, and I don't seem to be able to find the answers." I looked the young man in the eye and said, "You must simply believe; you must have child-like faith, not childish faith. Basically God said it, and we believe it, so that settles it. Simple faith will give you liberty and freedom."

That young man walked away with a beautiful smile on his face. I suggested he go and ask his girlfriend to forgive him. I told him to stop asking so many questions, because we are not God, we are merely His creation. God is in heaven and we are on earth. Why do we have the audacity or think we have the authority to question our Creator? Let's simply believe. Simple belief allows us to glide and soar on the thermals just like that eagle – carefree and fulfilled because that is how God intended it to be.

John 3 talks about Nicodemus. Nicodemus came to Jesus by night and asked Him, "What must a man do to inherit eternal life?" Jesus said that he had to be born again and make a new start. Nicodemus was an intellectual, a member of the elite "Sanhedrin". The Sanhedrin was the ruling body of elders in Israel at that time.

Nicodemus asked Jesus a second question: "How can a fully grown man go back into his mother's womb again?" In John 3:5, Jesus says, "Unless one is born of water and the Spirit, he cannot enter the kingdom of God." In verse 7, Jesus goes on to say, "Do not marvel that I said to you, 'You must be born again'." The important verse is verse 8 where Jesus says, "The *wind* blows where it wishes, and you hear the sound of it, but cannot tell where it comes from and where it goes" (emphasis added).

Nicodemus then asks Jesus, "How can these things be?" (verse 9). Jesus replies, "Are you the teacher of Israel, and do not know these things? Most assuredly, I say to you, We speak what We know and testify what We have seen, and you do not receive Our witness. If I have told you earthly things and you do not believe, how will you believe if I tell you heavenly things?" (verses 10–12).

We see that nothing has changed from the time Jesus walked on the earth until now. There are still men who choose to disagree and who choose to challenge God. It is a most fearful thing to fall into the hands of the living God. Why is it that we are prepared to believe anything else, but when it comes to spiritual things, we harden our hearts?

I think of that poor soul, the man bound to his wheelchair, who wrote a best-selling book trying to explain away spiritual things and instead explained how the world was created by a chemical explosion! I do not condemn this poor man; I just feel desperately sorry for him. He is like the Muscovy Duck that runs up and down his wire coop. He is fat because he has plenty of food to eat, but his wings no longer work. He cannot fly although he thinks he can. He runs up and down the coop making a quacking noise, as he watches the Spur-winged Goose fly overhead. The goose might not have as much food to eat as his muscovy cousin, but he is free. He may be lean, but he is enjoying life to the full, exercising what God has given him.

So many people are sitting on the fence, not prepared to get into the middle of the river and enjoy the full bounty – the power and the blessing of the Holy Spirit. It is so sad to see. All these people have to do is to get off the fence, and the Holy Spirit promises that He will do the rest.

That is what Peter – the rock, the big fisherman, the leader of the pack – did. Peter promised Jesus that he would never leave Him, that he would not run away and betray Him. In fact Peter said to Jesus that he would fight for Him and protect Him. Jesus responded with much compassion and told Peter that he would in fact deny Him three times before the cock crowed. And that is exactly what took place. Peter ran away after denying his Master – like a rat running into the sewer in the middle of the night. The Bible says, "He went out and wept bitterly" (Matthew 26:75).

Peter must have felt terribly wretched because he loved Jesus so much. He did not have the courage or the power to understand that Jesus would not forsake him or deny him in his time of great trial. Peter ran away from the only person in the world who could really help him. How often do you and I do that? We try everything in our own power and only when all has failed and we have no hope do we turn to God. This is such a dishonour to God.

Peter was baptized by the Holy Spirit, along with the other apostles, in the Upper Room. I have been to the Upper Room in Jerusalem. Some sceptics say that it wasn't the actual site, but that is of no consequence to me because it is located in that vicinity and most likely looked very similar to the original location.

The apostles had been cornered there. The Roman soldiers were hunting them down like wild animals and they were consumed with fear. They had no way of escape, they were at their wits' end and there was no hope. Their leader had been taken away and crucified.

The apostles had seen Jesus alive, three days after He had been crucified. Jesus told them to go to Jerusalem to wait there. He said, "You shall receive power when the Holy Spirit has come upon you; and you shall be

> He came like a rushing, mighty wind and baptized every one of them.

witnesses for Me in Jerusalem, and in all Judea and Samaria, and to the end of the earth" (Acts 1:8). That is exactly what the apostles did – they waited, and the Holy Spirit did not fail them. He came like a rushing, mighty wind and baptized every one of them.

The reaction was immediate, the Bible says. The apostles went out into the streets and witnessed for Jesus. Peter heard people from the street mocking the apostles and saying they were drunk. Peter addressed the people, people that were from every nation under the sun. He said, "These are not drunk, as you suppose, since it is only the third hour of the day" (9 a.m.) (Acts 2:15).

Peter proceeded to preach the gospel to the people, openly and at the cost of his own life. He did not hold back and was without fear and trepidation. Peter spoke with love, boldness, and authority and the Bible says that the number saved that day was about three thousand people. Only the power of God could have transformed that mortal fisherman from a deserter into a hero.

Jesus asked Peter three times, "Do you love Me?" And Peter answered the Lord and said, "Yes, Lord, You know I love You." By the third time Peter must have been weeping and so said: "Lord, You know all things." Jesus responded, "Feed My sheep" (John 21:17).

Peter's Landing is my favourite place in Israel. It is a place where I feel the Holy Spirit tangibly. There are steps at the water's edge of the Lake of Galilee, cut out of rock. Historians say that this is the place where Jesus stood two thousand years ago and said, "Children, have you any food?" (John 21:5). The response was, "No." Jesus then says, "Cast your net on the right side of the boat." Miraculously, the fishermen pulled up a great many fish and the nets did not break – another miracle (see John 21:6).

John recognized the voice and said to Peter, "It is the Lord!" (John 21:7). Peter was so overwhelmed that he jumped out of the boat, and, trying to put his coat on, he swam and waded until he got to the shore. It must have been a misty morning and that is when Jesus challenged Peter to feed His sheep. In spite of Peter's denial, in spite of the blasphemy, the Lord still loved Peter very much and had His hand firmly upon the big fisherman.

The Lord's calling is irrevocable. We need to follow through with the calling, but just like Peter, we cannot do it in our own strength. We need the empowering of the Holy Spirit to complete the Great Commission that the Lord has called us to.

> We need the empowering of the Holy Spirit to complete the Great Commission that the Lord has called us to.

After the Upper Room experience, Peter became the head of the church. He led from the front and was a great example. He was a mighty man for God from that point forward. He followed the same road as the apostle Paul – he became a martyr like so many of the early believers of Christ. Paul was beheaded in Rome because he was a Roman citizen. Peter was crucified like all the others who were not Roman by identification. The legend goes that Peter asked to be crucified upside down because he did not feel worthy to die like his Saviour.

What amazing love, what amazing power, what amazing courage from a man who did not even want to be identified with Jesus! What caused this incredible change of heart? He had been filled and empowered by meeting God's Holy Spirit in the Upper Room.

SEVEN

Obeying the Holy Spirit

After my encounter with the Holy Spirit at En-Gedi, I resolved, by the grace of God, to never apologize for the Holy Spirit who lives in me.

I never want to feel ashamed of the beautiful new language that I received from God. This language gives me such liberty to worship God. There is no more fear of man that inhibits me or prevents me from fulfilling what Father God has commissioned me to carry out for Him.

The Holy Spirit revealed Himself to me simply and in such a majestic way. Of what benefit is it to our fellow man to be singing and speaking in a foreign tongue? There is very little benefit, unless, as Paul says, an interpretation comes with it.

I find speaking in another language very special. My human mind does not understand, but my heart does and so does the heart of God. The devil can have no part of this conversation; he cannot sow evil thoughts into my mind when I am communing with God. The devil cannot interfere with my worship time with God, because he does not understand what I am singing about. There are so many beautiful benefits to believing and receiving the gift of the Holy Spirit.

Receiving the Holy Spirit has nothing to do with salvation. Jesus said that a man needs to be born again and he will enter the kingdom of heaven. The baptism of the Holy Spirit provides us with weapons that we can use in this world to defend ourselves and to liberate and free the captives.

At times when I have received phone calls requesting prayer, the message was unclear and all I could make out was, "Please pray!" I had no idea what I need to pray about. If I were to pray in my natural tongue, my prayer would be short because I don't know what I'm praying for. However, in my heavenly language I can pray at length, knowing that my prayers are being heard and understood by Father God, and answered.

Later, I have received a phone call to say the person in question was healed, set free, or delivered, the situation resolved, whatever the case may be. Likewise, singing in that new language is so refreshing and edifying. I love to sing in our natural language, too – I just love the old hymns and choruses.

> In my heavenly language I can pray at length, knowing that my prayers are being heard and understood.

I remember returning from a long overseas trip. I was tired from ministry and travelling so I decided to go for a slow, long run. I don't run far and I don't run fast. On this particular day I decided to go for a 12 kilometre run, but after running about 6 kilometres I started to feel weary. So I began to sing in the heavenly tongue God had given to me; it felt like a tonic. I found myself picking up my pace and enjoying every moment of the rest of my run.

John 14:16 speaks about this. Jesus said that He would pray to the Father and He would send us a Helper (*Parakletos*). He would abide with us forever, even the Spirit of truth whom the world could not receive. In verse 18, Jesus says that He won't leave us orphans and that He will come to us. The Holy Spirit does exactly that.

There are times when I am sitting on the other side of the world in a hotel room, waiting for the next meeting to start. I feel lonely; I miss Jill and wonder what she is doing, especially if I haven't been able to reach her by phone.

It is at times like this that the Helper comforts and encourages me. Jesus Christ is concerned about our every need. Before He left earth, He said He would make sure we had everything we need. The only thing that prevents us from receiving His full blessing is unbelief. We need to cast aside all our worldly intelligence and trust Him. He will never let us down.

About thirty years ago, I was a relatively new Christian. We had moved down to South Africa from Zambia a couple of years before. We had purchased the farm Shalom which my sons have since taken over. I remember obtaining a seed maize contract from one of the biggest seed companies in the country. When planting this crop, the timing is crucial due to the cross pollination of the varieties and in order for the crop to succeed. We couldn't wait for the right time; we had to plant as soon as possible because we only had a little two-row planter. To get this large crop planted meant that time was of the essence. These days, farmers are using fifteen- and twenty-row planters; it was a miracle that we were able to get our crop in when we did.

That particular year, I decided to wait for the rain to come. Time passed and the rain didn't come. I felt the Holy Spirit tell me to go ahead and plant the maize crop into dry land. Elijah the prophet had told King Ahab the same thing – it had not rained for three and a half years in Israel at that stage. He told King Ahab to gird up his loins and get back to Jerusalem because the rain was coming. Shortly after Elijah's prophesy, Israel experienced a deluge of rain. We started to plant in the dust and any farmer will tell you that it is absolute suicide to do something like that.

Seed that falls in moist parts of the field will germinate and seed that falls in drier parts of the field will lie there until the rain comes. The seed that has germinated in the moist soil does not have enough moisture to push through to the surface and begins to rot. The bottom line is that after "dry land" planting, one needs good rain otherwise you will have a disaster on your hands.

I went ahead by the instruction of the Holy Spirit and

started to sow good seed. I planted and I planted and still there was not a sign of rain. My neighbours were watching over the fence, and were probably thinking that I had really lost it this time! It got progressively drier and still no sign of rain. The dust became thicker and the wind blew; still no sign of rain. I had to get goggles for my tractor drivers, because they just couldn't see where they were driving, the dust was so bad. But by faith in God's Holy Word and through the direction of the Holy Spirit, we continued to plant.

We had planted almost half the acreage before the long-awaited rain arrived. When it came, it poured with great ferocity. The fields became so water-logged and muddy that the tractors could not get in to plant. The neighbours were starting to realize that maybe I wasn't so mad! The seed started to push through the ground and those faint green lines were starting to show – a sight that will always bless my soul because we know that it is only God who can create new life.

Some farmers had not even prepared their lands, let alone planted. The rain just kept on coming. We would get one or two days of hot, dry weather, which allowed us to fertilize and spray the crops. That glorious crop just kept on growing. With the abundant rain and sun, we had a magnificent bumper crop. Some of our neighbours had nothing to reap because by the time they had managed to get their crops planted, the prime growing period had passed.

Some people said we were "lucky" – I don't know what that word means, but I do know what it is to be "blessed". God blesses those who are obedient and simply do what He says. When we follow God's directives some people will even consider us to be wise men and women. Don't harden your heart; if God speaks, make the relative adjustments in your life.

> God blesses those who are obedient and simply do what He says.

"Pride always comes before a fall" is a saying we all have heard many times before. In 1 Peter 5:5, the Lord says that He resists the proud but gives grace to the humble. It is often pride that blocks us from allowing the Holy Spirit to take full control of our lives. It is also the fear of man – something I have to constantly deal with in my own life. Foolish, arrogant pride!

I was preaching in Pretoria and a man brought a Doctor of Divinity to the meeting to listen to the encounter we had had with the Holy Spirit at En-Gedi. This theologian is a highly intelligent, competent believer; he has many different degrees in theology and could even be a professor of the faith. However, he did tend to shy away from the gifts of the Holy Spirit.

We showed the film clip of the visitation of the Holy Spirit at En-Gedi and I gave a first-hand account of what took place. I said that we needed to move our reasoning from our heads to our hearts. We need to allow the Holy Spirit to speak into our hearts, because head knowledge helps no one; it is the love of Christ in a man's heart that will change the world.

I spoke about the love of God that transformed the life of that great American revivalist and former lawyer, Charles Finney. It penetrated his heart so powerfully that he cried out to the Lord while he was lying in a forest, "Lord, if you do not stop this love which is penetrating my heart, You will literally kill me."

The love of God can be so overwhelming that an ordinary mortal man cannot comprehend all of it. The Doctor of Divinity broke down and wept at the end of the service. He realized that He had missed it completely, but we trust that now his ministry will really take off and bloom because he has had a real experience with the Holy Spirit.

There was a man in the Bible called Saul of Tarsus. He was a member of the Sanhedrin and a highly intelligent Jew. He regarded Jesus Christ as an imposter and spent all his time hunting down and killing followers of Jesus. He was determined to obliterate Christianity from the face of the earth. He was a man who reasoned with his head, but it was only when he was knocked off his horse on the way to Damascus, that he met with the living God.

God asks Saul, "Why are you persecuting Me?" "Who are You, Lord?" Saul asks the voice speaking to him from the clear blue sky. "I am Jesus" (Acts 9:4–5).

I believe that he was born again and baptized by the Holy Spirit at that very moment. I believe that Paul received the gifts available to believers all at once. If you look at Paul's track record, he performed signs, wonders, and miracles; he prophesied; he had incredible strength; and he was totally fearless.

People were unable to put this giant of the faith down. He was shipwrecked, he was stoned, he was beaten many times and left for dead and yet he carried on preaching the Gospel with untiring faith. He also wrote two thirds of the New Testament. Paul definitely received power from on high, and my prayer was that the young Doctor of Divinity who attended the service would also receive this power from God.

There is a beautiful Scripture in Zechariah 4:6 that says, "Not by might nor by power, but by My Spirit, says the Lord of Hosts."

This Scripture has become so real to me. The only way we are going to overcome and finish strong in these trying times is by allowing the Holy Spirit to come into our lives and to work through us. We need to put our pride in our back pocket and allow the Holy Spirit to use us to perform signs and wonders and miracles. We need to ask God to take all doubt from us.

That is exactly what Billy Graham did. He put his Bible on a stump of wood in the middle of a forest and said to God that he was choosing to believe, by faith, the many things he did not understand, and that he believed the Bible to be true, from cover to cover. The result of that act of faith is evident. There is not a modern-day evangelist in the world today who has spoken to as many people as Billy Graham. He has touched the world through his simple faith in the Son of God.

EIGHT

A Great Faith

"The eyes of the Lord run to and fro throughout the whole earth, to show Himself strong on behalf of those whose heart is loyal to Him" (2 Chronicles 16:9).

God does not need our intellect; He needs our trust. He needs us to believe in Him and He will do the rest. Faith comes by hearing, and hearing by the Word of God (see Romans 10:17). Spending more time with the Lord will make us men and women of great faith. It is then that we can offer our services to Jesus without any doubt.

Before leaving for the Feast of Tabernacles in Israel, I spent time with the Lord and wrote a few things down in a little notebook. I would like to share these thoughts with you.

29/09/2012 Israel trip

"Man of Prayer"

Psalm 109:4: "But I give myself to prayer." Master, the more You open doors for me in Your kingdom work, the more I desire to walk closer to You, to spend time in prayer, in meditation and in Your Holy Word. Then I can be ready for whatever You call me to. Amen.

29/09/2012 Jerusalem

Nothing short of Revival will suffice! Master, before I go home to be with You, I desire to see with my carnal eyes, full blown REVIVAL. I have such a burden for the USA; please use me. But I do realize that if I am to be used by You, I must be prepared to spend time in solitude in Your presence so that I will not fail You when I am needed.

Please help me to pace myself better, Master, so that I am ready to bring Your Holy Word to the lost, the poor, and the needy, and to this very city (Jerusalem). You know what it is like to be lonely, to drink of the cup, and You did it, Lord Jesus. The wonderful news for us is that You had the victory in the end, and so shall I. Because You live, I can face tomorrow and complete the Great Commission. We can do it, Lord, and furthermore it is the mandate I received from You all those years ago in Greytown – to go into all the world and preach the Gospel to all nations telling them exactly what You said:

- The time is fulfilled
- The kingdom of God is at hand
- Repent
- Believe in the Gospel.

"I must work the works of Him who sent Me while it is day; the night is coming when no one can work" (John 9:4). A much greater urgency is needed! "My soul, wait silently for God alone, for my expectation [hope] is from Him" (Psalm 62:5). When You place a burden on my heart, You also give me the means to do something about it.

The warrior is made on the battlefield, so I shall not be the one to draw back. "Not by might nor by power, but by My Spirit, says the Lord of Hosts" (Zechariah 4:6). There are no other plans, only Your ones. Show Your glory tonight, Lord Holy Spirit, please, I beg You. May it be Your will only that is done today at En-Gedi. Take Your glory, Lord.

Jesus, You are waiting for me at En-Gedi, nothing less than REVIVAL. It is the power we need. You are speaking to me so clearly at the moment through Your Holy Word. The Upper Room experience is so needed in the world today. Acts 2 is so explicit, but we, the church of the twenty-first century, often overlook the Holy Spirit and by doing so I believe we offend Him greatly.

We forget to acknowledge Him. He is holy and will not and cannot work with backsliders or with people who do not believe. Even the disciples cried out to Jesus to please increase their

> I believe that Jesus Christ is the only begotten Son of God.

faith. We are not going to make it on our own. We need help desperately, so let us call upon the Comforter.

I believe that Jesus Christ is the only begotten Son of God. I believe that He is a weatherman. He can turn water into choice wine as well. He can raise the dead, heal the leper, walk on the water, and I know that He is alive. He is the very One who told us that we need to be born again, baptized in water and filled with His Holy Spirit. We need to walk by faith and not by sight (2 Corinthians 5:7 and Mark 11:22). That only comes to us when we spend lots of time in God's Holy Word.

02/10/2012

Last night, I spoke just outside the Jaffa Gate, Jerusalem. Seven hundred South African pilgrims attended. I was very emotional and full of Holy Spirit fire. I said to the Lord in my prayer time that I would never, ever compromise His Word again, or any message that He gives me to preach to His children. I will not ignore His sovereign presence in any service I would take again.

A message had been prepared for the meeting before I had even left South Africa. However, after the previous night's encounter with the Holy Spirit, I waived all my notes and just started speaking about the supernatural encounter we had had at En-Gedi. I poured out my heart, sharing in detail what had taken place at the meeting – how the fire had come down, how people were saved and filled to overflowing by the supernatural presence of God. I made an altar call and asked those who wished to be baptized in the Holy Spirit to come forward.

Although more reserved than the night before, they responded. There was a deep reverence and a godly fear present. I truly believe everyone was touched in a special way. I think this was the first stand made by a lot of conservative folk, and I am trusting that by the end of their pilgrimage, they will have met You, Lord Holy Spirit, and will be able to communicate with You in their new language.

Lord Holy Spirit, I do love You so. Please guide me with regard to making decisions for the future; I need divine direction. Thank You for the newfound love and relationship I have in and through You. It feels like I've been born all over again – I am so content today and fulfilled in every aspect of my life. I'm so at peace.

Thank You, Jesus, for reminding me that I am not alone because You have sent me Your Holy Spirit. I intend to never neglect my relationship with Him again. The sheer power I experienced on Sunday night at En-Gedi is so hard for me to put into words. I feel so tender towards You today, Father God. What a mighty God we serve. You are so real to me. It is important for me to rest in You now, to come aside and to meditate on what happened in Israel over these past days.

> The name of Jesus has been lifted up, for He has touched so many lives and changed people forever, especially me.

The name of Jesus has been lifted up, for He has touched so many lives and changed people forever, especially me. You have put a new passion in my heart for signs, wonders, and miracles. I am so excited to be in Your service, Lord Jesus. The best is still coming; I feel it in my spirit, Holy Spirit. I am not content where I am at the moment, for there is so much more. The most precious thing for me is the intimacy I feel I have with You at this time, and I am determined not to let it pass by me again.

Oswald Chambers, that anointed Scottish preacher, made it very clear how important it is to have the Lord Holy Spirit working actively in my life, if I am to complete this journey He has called me to.

In his devotional *My Utmost for His Highest*, Chambers says that Peter, the big fisherman, had to come to the end of himself before God could use him in supernatural exploits. He had to realize what a pathetic case he was without God's power in his life. He had denied Jesus three times; he had cursed and even blasphemed Him. Peter's so-called self-sufficiency had been trashed; he would not be able to rely on himself again. He was destitute spiritually and had no self-confidence left.

So what happened? He was completely taken over by the Holy Spirit. From that moment on, He became a totally new character, a different person. When he laid his hands upon the sick in Jesus' name, they were instantly healed. When his life was threatened, he felt no fear. He was so bold that at the end of his short life, when he was about to be crucified by the Romans, he asked to be crucified upside down because he did not feel worthy to die like his Saviour. What a miraculous change in a man's life – only God can do that. Peter went from a coward to becoming a glorious martyr.

Master, I shall spend quality time and quantity time with You. When I serve Your children, I want to do it with all my heart and soul. Please help me to not "cast my pearls before swine" (Matthew 7:6), but to only share what has taken place in my life through your Holy Spirit, with those who really want to know. I am determined to give my beloved Holy Spirit more place from now on. I don't want to hold back or to apologize. You are alive and are here to comfort, to help, and to perform miracles. I am available for whatever You want from me.

I will not be anxious about anything. I will be still and wait on You. I will climb my mountain, Holy Spirit, with You by my side, and I will conquer it, too. By Your love I will go the whole way – I will scale my mountain to the top. There is no place that is sweeter than to be in Your presence having my Quiet Time. There is no turning back now. I am going through to the end and I know I am going to make it.

Let that REVIVAL start in me, Holy Spirit. Fill me, please, with the fire of Your love for the lost. I intend to remain faithful to You, Lord Jesus, to the end. More of You, Holy Spirit, and none of me.

16/10/2012

Two weeks after my encounter with the Holy Spirit at En-Gedi, Israel, I was called to an emergency rally at the Olympus Stadium in Rustenburg. Miners had gone on strike and the police had tried to contain them. Things had gotten out of control and over thirty striking miners had been shot dead by the police. As a result, all the other surrounding mines closed and the mineworkers started to strike.

The town of Rustenburg was in a state of confusion and fear. A Christian campaign was organized at the stadium, to pray for peace. The event was called "New Beginnings". The Scripture verse used was 2 Chronicles 7:14: "If My people who are called by My name will humble themselves, and pray and seek My face, and turn from their wicked ways, I will hear from heaven, and will forgive their sin and heal their land."

My diary reads as follows:

Master, I am now beginning to understand why You allowed me to experience the En-Gedi encounter. It is so that I may be courageous and be able to speak the truth in love and power. I need not feel afraid because I know You are with me at all times.

"Fear is generated by unbelief, and unbelief strengthened by fear. Nothing can cure us of fear till God cures us of unbelief" (Francis Burkitt).

How true that statement is. I was privileged to have had that encounter with You, my Lord Holy Spirit. It has increased my faith in God no end.

18/10/2012

I am on my way to Rustenburg on Saturday morning. I spent yesterday with Jesus. He has given me a clear mandate to deliver to the people. I had confirmation from Reinhard Bonnke to preach nothing but the undiluted Gospel. I'm in God's army, full-time, so I had better be in good shape. I must forget about myself and start shaping up for Jesus. I must decrease, so Jesus can increase in me.

Master, may I never block the way so people can't see You. Please, Holy Spirit, ensure that I never touch God's glory, even unintentionally. There is no room in God's army for idolatry or man-pleasing. I'm laying it all down for Jesus.

19/10/2012

If I have to die, then let it be for a worthwhile cause. There is only one worthwhile cause and that is to deliver a mandate from God (Ezekiel 3:10–11).

Tomorrow, Master, I ask only one thing: more courage to execute the duty You have given me to do, to preach the acceptable year of the Lord and to call people back to God by telling them the truth in love. They must be born again, repent of their wicked ways, call upon the name of Jesus Christ, and believe for total victory.

NINE

New Beginnings

The day for the Rustenburg campaign arrived, but the weather was poor. We were supposed to fly to Rustenburg, about an hour and a half flying time from the farm. There was so much rain that Tommy, my assistant for the campaign, drove down from Johannesburg to collect me. We left in the early hours of the morning to drive up north. We stopped in Johannesburg, where I had been asked to dedicate a church on their twentieth anniversary. The fire of God fell and many souls came to Christ. There was much reconciliation and healing that took place.

After the meeting, we drove to the airport and flew to Rustenburg. On the outskirts of Rustenburg, we were put on a helicopter and flown to the stadium. The crowd was so expectant; we could feel the electricity in the air. I got out the helicopter and was met by Rory Alec, the

CEO of GOD TV. He had flown out from England for the event. This meeting was of special importance to Rory as he originally came from Rustenburg. He interviewed me, then I walked straight out onto the platform and started preaching.

Normally, I have an opportunity to sit quietly and sing one or two hymns before I am introduced to speak. But this was not the case. I walked up the stairs and onto the stage, a microphone was handed to me, and I was told to "Go for it!" It took me a few minutes to collect myself, so I started off by singing a Zulu hymn. That settled the crowd, a mix of black and white, all desperate for solutions. I delivered the "mandate" to the people; I don't think I could even call it a sermon. The mandate I received from God addressed three critical issues:

- *The greed in the country:* I challenged the mine management to put their hands deeper into their pockets and to pay a fair day's wage for a fair day's work. I also reminded the mine workers on strike that the Bible says that a lazy man does not deserve to eat. Mining is an extremely hard way to earn a living. I've been down a mine once in my life, and never again!
- *Respect for life:* I challenged the strikers to have more respect for life. The violence had to stop, and they needed to lay down their arms and return to work. The harder they worked, the more money would be generated and then hopefully the mine management could pay them all a better wage. I re-

minded them of their loved ones at home, whether it be in Lesotho, Zambia, Malawi, or Mozambique. Their families were desperately waiting for money to buy food and clothing for their children.

- *Apathy among believers:* I emphasized this point the most – talking with no action, and praying and doing nothing achieves little. Prayer is a verb: once the church prays, it must put the prayer of faith into action.

While I was preaching, a group of "mighty men" were in one of the boxes in the stadium, interceding for God to undertake and protect us. I stated that the church was responsible for the unrest and the strike.

If we look at the key Scripture, "If My people who are called by My name..." (2 Chronicles 7:14), it refers to the believer. That was not happening, so obviously we as believers were not doing our work as the land was anything but healed. We needed to start again; we needed a "New Beginning". I felt that I was constantly being empowered by the Holy Spirit during the meeting; something I had never felt before.

One of the turning points of the day came from a little black girl. She was a few years old and I found out later that she was an orphan, adopted by a white pastor and his wife. The little girl didn't go to strangers and was shy by nature. While I was preaching, I walked past her and picked her up in my arms, to give her a hug – I love children and have nine grandchildren. The little girl put her head on my shoulder and wrapped her arms around my neck, just like one of my grandchildren would. She was wearing a pretty floral dress and a little pair of sandals; she was a really beautiful child. I carried her around the platform while I completed my sermon.

We concluded the meeting by singing the national anthem. I got down on my knees and thanked God for changed lives, for unity, and for reconciliation. The photographers took a photograph of me on my knees, with this little girl sitting next to me, holding my finger in her hand.

This was the message of reconciliation, when people become as little children and embrace the Holy Spirit as the only source of power to deliver a nation. Once we had finished singing the anthem, we called people to the front and challenged them to trust God for a change in the nation. The stands emptied and the whole crowd gathered around the platform; it was a wonderful sight. We prayed together, black and white, male and female, young and old.

We received reports in the days that followed that on the Monday morning many of the striking miners walked back to the mines – they didn't even wait for their buses. They reported for duty and the mine management was overwhelmed because they had not expected them to return. There have been pockets of dissension since, but by and large there has been a change in the heavenlies, and I put that down to the mercy of God.

A week after the event, one of the major unions in the country staged a meeting at the same stadium. The stadium erupted in absolute chaos, the police were brought in, and tear gas was used to try to restore peace.

Demonstrators were running wild, to the point that some of the senior police officers called the organizers of our New Beginnings event, and wanted to know how we had managed to hold such an orderly meeting. There had been no antagonism, no demonstrations, and no anger at our meeting, just the love of God. Why is it so often that we dig in our heels when the Lord Jesus wants to use us to heal His people?

> Why is it so often we dig in our heels when the Lord Jesus wants to use us to heal His people?

A few years ago I had the privilege of speaking at a beautiful old church, which was just up the road from St Paul's Cathedral in London, England. It is called City Temple and it was built by a great preacher by the name of Joseph Parker. In the nineteenth century, Joseph Parker and Baptist preacher Charles Haddon Spurgeon took London by storm for the Lord Jesus Christ. Spurgeon was a Baptist and Parker was from the Congregational Church; they were both men who really loved God and were used very powerfully by Him. I picked up a quotation the other day from a devotional book written over two hundred years ago by Joseph Parker, in which he writes:

> If we, as the Church, do not get back to spiritual visions, glimpses of Heaven, and an awareness of a greater glory and life, we will lose our faith. Our altar will become nothing but

cold, empty stone, never blessed by a visit from Heaven. This is the world's need today – people who have seen their Lord.

We saw the Lord in all His glory at En-Gedi. I read Jeremiah 51:15–16 the other morning:

> He has made the earth by His power; He has established the world by His wisdom, and stretched out the heaven by His understanding. When He utters His voice – there is a multitude of waters in the heavens: 'He causes the vapors to ascend from the ends of the earth; He makes lightnings for the rain; He brings the wind out of His treasuries.'

This is such a beautiful Scripture and confirms that God is the weatherman.

I think it was Derek Prince who said there is so much power in personal testimony. When a man relays a personal testimony, you cannot argue with him. You can either agree or you can disagree, but you cannot argue because you were not there.

A word that has become very prominent in my vocabulary is the word "expedient". It means suitable, or appropriate, convenient and practical. A verse that has become very real to me since En-Gedi is John 16:7 (KJV): "Nevertheless I tell you the truth; it is expedient for you that I go away: for if I go not away, the Comforter will not come unto you; but if I depart, I will send Him unto you."

Jesus knew that He could only be at one place at one time because He was God but He was also man. He knew that His Holy Spirit could be at all places at all times. In *The Message*, John 16:7 reads,

> I didn't tell you this earlier because I was with you every day. But now I am on my way to the One who sent Me. Not one of you has asked, 'Where are you going?' Instead, the longer I've talked, the sadder you've become. So let me say it again, this truth: It's better for you that I leave. If I don't leave, the Friend won't come. But if I go, I'll send him to you.

The Bible also says in Proverbs 18:24 that there is a friend who sticks closer than a brother.

I read a Bible commentary about this very passage, which commented on the Holy Spirit coming on Jesus' departure. It said, "... A gift awaiting Jesus' departure". The Lord was not going to leave us empty-handed; He was sending us a gift, again referring to the power of personal testimony.

I received a letter from Ivo Wüst, a very dear brother in Christ, who wrote:

> ... Having heard testimonies at the Shalom church from both Angus and Clive Tedder, his assistant who accompanied him, on the miraculous manifestations of the Holy Spirit at En-Gedi, at the Feast of Tabernacles, I was aware of what transpired on that momentous occasion. They gave us, the local church, an emotional indication of what the impact of this supernatural manifestation had on their lives, and on those who witnessed it.

Ivo and his wife, Joan, were having devotions and they experienced what can only be called a God incident. They had been reading systematically through their Bible and had got to the book of Ezekiel chapter 47. Verses 7 and 12 made reference to En-Gedi and they were convinced that they should share this verse with me to encourage me. It speaks about the Dead Sea being changed from the saltiest, most mineral-rich stretch of water, to a lake of healing waters around which trees will grow and in which fish will live – a multitude of fish so great that fishermen will be able to spread their nets in the lake. Ezekiel 47:10 states:

> It shall be that fishermen will stand by it from En Gedi to En Eglaim; they will be places for spreading their nets. Their fish will be of the same kinds as the fish of the Great Sea, exceedingly many.

Verse 12 says:

> Along the bank of the river... will grow all kinds of trees used for food; their leaves will not wither, and their fruit will not fail. They will bear fruit every month, because their water flows from the sanctuary. Their fruit will be for food, and their leaves for medicine.

As Ivo shared this truth with me, I was totally amazed and encouraged. The river that will flow from Jerusalem down 400 metres into the Dead Sea will sweeten those waters so that fish and other life can live in the lake, with fruit trees growing on the banks. I was deeply touched by that testimony because there is nothing that can live at the Dead Sea. It hardly rains there and yet that night as we read Acts 2, not only did the wind blow like a tornado, but it also rained.

The beautiful parallel is that Jesus turns death into life, by His beautiful Holy Spirit being present. I was very thankful for Ivo's obedience and timeliness. With God, as we can see through His Living Word, nothing is impossible. Abraham and Sarah asked in Genesis 18:14, "Is there anything too hard for the Lord?" The answer is a definite, "No!" Absolutely nothing is too hard for God. Abraham was one hundred years old, Sarah just a few years younger and yet she gave birth to a beautiful baby boy: Isaac.

The evening at En-Gedi, a supernatural river flowed from the heart of God into each one of those four and a half thousand pilgrims. God made dead hearts come alive. What God gave us needs to be shared with others all over the world. We are living in the last days and as time runs out, it's only the Holy Spirit who will save people in multitudes.

I've asked myself why the Holy Spirit would choose to manifest Himself as He did at the Dead Sea. The Dead Sea is the lowest point on earth

> We are living in the last days and as time runs out, it's only the Holy Spirit who will save people in multitudes.

and one of the hottest, there is no life there, the water is contaminated with salt and minerals, and it is deserted – why choose a place like that?

I asked myself, *Where was Jesus found when the Son of God walked the face of the earth? Was He found in a palace, in places of finery and luxury, with the wealthy?* No, He was found with the widows and orphans, among the poor and neglected. He was born in a stable; His cot was a feeding trough. He came from a very poor family and was born in a very humble village. Jesus could have been born in Caesar's palace in Rome or in Pharaoh's palace in Egypt. He could have been taught by the greatest teachers from Greece; yet His teacher was the Holy Spirit and His humble home a carpenter's shop.

He was educated by observing life; He understood hunger, poverty, and disease. Jesus said that He had not come for those who were well, but for those who were sick. Maybe that is why we had the privilege of meeting the Holy Spirit at the lowest point and the most lifeless place on earth.

In my walk with the Lord, I have experienced how He will show us something in the physical first, and then in the spiritual. I firmly believe that one of the reasons for the choice of En-Gedi as the location was to remind us that Jesus came to save all men and that He has always had a heart for the weak, the needy, and those who have lost all hope.

Our mission in life should be to be effective wherever God puts us. Some of the neediest people on earth are rich folk. They may be rich when it comes to money and power, but they are poor in spirit and so lifeless. Caring for celebrities is a specialized ministry. Let us not forget those who are in prison, in hospital, those who have no parents or have no food to eat. It is these people of whom Jesus said, "Inasmuch as ye have done it unto one of the least of these my brethren, ye have done it unto me" (Matthew 25:40 KJV).

TEN

Mighty Men

Duncan Campbell, a man God used in the Hebrides Revival, was asked why God only used him in one Revival. His answer was straightforward. He said that it was because physically he would not have been able to handle another Revival, because it takes so much out of a person.

It was July 2003 and I was extremely tired. We had had a very busy season and my wife, Jill, and I had gone up to the Mhkuze Game Reserve in northern Zululand to have a break.

It was the second or third morning, and I was having my Quiet Time in the beautiful African bushveld. It was so peaceful. We were in a little bungalow hidden in the undergrowth and it was shady and quiet.

We had purposefully booked out of season so there was hardly anyone else at the camp. I was meditating on the goodness of the Lord and I felt the Lord speaking to my heart as I read the Scriptures. It is important to have a regular Quiet Time.

I felt the Lord speak to me in an almost audible voice. I was reading from Revelation 2:2–5:

> "I know your works, your labor, your patience, and that you cannot bear those who are evil. And you have tested those who say they are apostles and are not, and have found them liars; and you have persevered and have patience and have labored for My name's sake and have not become weary. Nevertheless I have this against you, that you have left your first love. Remember therefore from where you have fallen; repent and do the first works, or else I will come to you quickly and remove your lampstand from its place – unless you repent."

I wrote in the margin of my Bible, *Turning point in the work of God, in my life, July 2003, Mkuze.* I was absolutely devastated because I had thought I was doing so much for the Lord. I was preaching all over the world; I was writing books, making TV programmes, writing columns for magazines, speaking in sporting stadiums and indoor arenas – there was not much more I could do.

I shared with Jill what I believed God was telling me and spent the rest of the holiday in deep contemplation and meditation. I felt the Lord wanted me to cancel all of my preaching appointments for the rest of the year.

The Lord spoke to me and said, "Repent, stop what you are doing and do what you did at first. Otherwise I will come and remove the candlestick from you." This I understood to be the light, the Holy Spirit.

Any evangelist will tell you that to get onto a platform and preach to a vast audience, without the Holy Spirit, is suicidal. At large outdoor events, people don't have to sit still and listen to your message – if there is no Holy Spirit anointing, people get up and walk out! This is unlike the traditional church setting where people sit politely to the end of your message, whether they like it or not.

> To get onto a platform and preach to a vast audience, without the Holy Spirit, is suicidal.

I chose to obey the instructions of God, for fear of offending the Holy Spirit and losing the anointing of God on my life. On return from our holiday, I cancelled all my preaching engagements for the year. The first miracle that took place, and left me amazed, was that none of the people were angry with me for cancelling – and some of these folk had booked me up to two years in advance.

There was unanimous support: "If that is what God has said, then who are we to argue? We will wait for the right timing." I remember sharing my decision with a fellow evangelist and I was so disappointed with his response. His reply was, "I could never do that!" I asked why. He replied, "If I had to cancel all my appointments for the year, I would starve." I thought to myself, *I am not a hireling. I am a son and I do not work for a wage; I work for my inheritance.*

"Obedience is better than sacrifice and to obey is better than the fat of rams," the Bible tells us. After cancelling all my appointments, I asked God to

> I am not a hireling. I am a son and I do not work for a wage; I work for my inheritance.

show me what to do next. I didn't want to just sit and do nothing!

I felt the Lord say clearly to my spirit, "Angus, I want you to mentor young men. I want you to father young men because we are sitting with a fatherless generation."

I thought the Lord wanted me to mentor five to ten men. So I sent out an email to a few people whom I knew and that was the sum total of my advertising.

Remember, I am an evangelist – I don't know how to advertise with handbills, posters, adverts on TV and radio. I did none of that and in a way I was putting a fleece before the Lord. It was a case of: *Lord, this is Your directive, so please will You bring the men?*

I was flabbergasted when two hundred and forty men arrived on the farm. We started on the Friday evening, ran the whole day of Saturday, and finished up on the Sunday. The women and children joined us on Sunday for the morning service. The men came to me at the end of the conference and asked whether there would be another "Mighty Men™" Conference the next year. I said I would pray about it, but they responded that they would be returning anyway! That was the start of the God-breathed Mighty Men™ phenomenon.

The next year we had six hundred men. They arrived from all over the country. They were men's men – no "weaklings" among them. There were businessmen, miners, farmers, professional sportsmen, teachers, and university students. We started on the Friday again. On the Saturday night I witnessed something I shall never forget as long as I live: we had a communion service that started at two o'clock and finished at eight that evening.

The meeting started in the heat of the day. The hall had no ceiling, just a tin roof; there was no air conditioning. We had fed the men a huge braai (barbeque) at lunch and I wondered how we were going to keep these men awake in such conditions! We closed the doors and there were six hundred of us in that confined area – it was a preacher's nightmare! I handed the meeting over to the Holy Spirit as I always do and I had one message left to share.

> We need to take action if we expect the Holy Spirit to use us.

The Holy Spirit took complete control of that meeting. I started to preach and saw some of the men start to doze off. I was speaking about being an ambassador for Christ; my point was that in order to be an ambassador for Christ, we cannot afford to have skeletons in our cupboards. We need to deal with issues, whether they be at home or at work, whether they may be trouble with our colleagues or problems with our kids. We need to take action if we expect the Holy Spirit to use us.

I stopped preaching and suggested we take a tea break. I closed my Bible and was prompted by the Holy Spirit to say that I felt there was a father and son in the meeting who needed to forgive each other and reconcile, before we went for tea. There was no response from the crowd of mature men and I repeated it a second time. There was still no acknowledgment from anyone. I was feeling a bit foolish and wondered whether I had heard the Holy Spirit correctly.

Once more I said, "Chaps, if there is somebody here..." and with that, a young man stood up on the one side of the hall. As he stood another, much older gentleman got out of his chair on the other side. The two started to walk towards each other.

I asked them to come onto the platform where they were reconciled in front of the large crowd of men. Much weeping and forgiveness took place and this opened the floodgates. Men started coming up onto the platform from all over the hall. This continued until after eight that night. The men were lined up around the hall, waiting to come onto the platform and ask God for forgiveness, in front of the crowd of witnesses.

I remember a policeman, now a full-time pastor, who came to the conference with his son. The son was sitting in the crowd and the policeman got up onto the platform, broke down, and told the men present that he had never publicly told his son that he was proud of him and loved him very much. The eighteen-year-old son got out of his seat and ran down the aisle to his dad; they hugged in the aisle and were reconciled instantly.

We found out afterwards that this young man had not made the first rugby team at school; he was struggling to even make the second team. But after his dad's affirmation that day, he stepped right into the first team squad at school and after he left school, he played semi-professional rugby. His life had been completely transformed. Revival must have fruit – there is no point in having a wonderful meeting and then it is all over. There must be fruit that one hears of even years later.

> Revival must have fruit – there is no point in having a wonderful meeting and then it is all over.

Another group of three young men came up onto the platform and spoke into the video camera. They spoke to their absent father through the camera and forgave him for the way he had treated their mother for many years. They broke down and wept and through tears of forgiveness told their dad that they loved him. There was not a dry eye in the building.

Another group of young South Africans got onto the platform with their dad, who had been divorced twice before. He asked his boys to forgive him for the hurt he had caused them through his failed marriages. They had their arms around him and were crying out, "Dad, we love you and forgive you!" This continued for hours.

> "Dad, we love you and forgive you!" This continued for hours.

Another farmer came up and repented before God; he had promised the Lord that he would build a church on his farm but had only got as far as laying the slab for the foundations. He said the Holy Spirit had convicted him to go back home after the conference and complete the building.

A wealthy businessman from Cape Town stepped up and confessed that he had not being paying his income tax, amounting to over R450,000 (that was a lot of money ten years ago – when this conference took place). He was going to pay the full amount on his return home.

At the end of the evening, representatives from two churches in the crowd came to the front. These two churches had been at loggerheads with each other; two groups of brave, pale-faced elders came to the front, seeking to forgive and forget and move forward together.

At the end of the meeting we had communion together. The Lord had told me to buy huge loaves of bread, which we had laid out on the table with litres of red grape juice in cups. We broke off large chunks of the loaves and with cups of grape juice in our hands, walked around and served each other, encouraging each other to finish the race in victory.

What took place was genuine forgiveness and real reconciliation. Grown men cried like babies and got rid of all kinds of fears and anxieties in an atmosphere of complete trust and understanding. There were many chains, shackles, and heavy burdens left at the altar that weekend. Men walked away free and forgiven, ready to continue the race with no handicaps.

The following year, 2004, we had over a thousand men. Every single year the crowd of men got bigger and eventually we trusted the Lord for five thousand men. We hired a five thousand-seater tent and seven and a half thousand men turned up. We were feeding the men ourselves, not taking collections at the meetings, and trusting the Lord to settle all our accounts. Miraculously, we would come out square at the end of each conference. That in itself was such a great testimony of God's faithful provision.

At one conference, just as the men were settling into the tent for the first session, the ladies came out of the kitchen in a panic. They had only prepared enough food for five thousand, meaning that there was only enough for two thirds of the men!

They asked me to tell the men to go easy on portions and I said I would. I got onto the stage and said, "Men, a message from the kitchen: eat as much as you can!" That's not a message you have to tell hungry young men twice! When the kitchen opened, there were men coming out with five or six bread rolls and plates heaped with meat and vegetables and pudding.

On the Sunday morning just before the last service was about to start, I was in my prayer room praying. My dear friend Peter Hull came in; he is such a humble servant of God. He was wearing a red bib, which indicated that he had been directing traffic. He came into my prayer room and tears were running down his face. I thought there might have been an accident and that somebody had been hurt.

Peter said, "Angus, I have just come from the kitchen and the ladies have just told me what has happened." We gave the men three meals: Friday night supper, and lunch and supper on Saturday. The men prepared their own breakfasts. Peter said that they had just counted the leftovers from the three meals served and there were thirty-six baskets. If we divided those baskets by the three meals served, that would mean there were twelve baskets left over per meal.

In the Bible, Jesus spoke to five thousand people and then He fed them with two fish and five barley loaves of bread. After the meal, the disciples collected twelve baskets of leftovers:

> When He [Jesus] had taken the five loaves and the two fish, He looked up to heaven, blessed and broke the loaves, and gave them to His disciples to set before them; and the two fish He divided among them all. So they all ate and were filled. And they took up twelve baskets full of fragments and of the fish (Mark 6:41–43).

That same miracle took place here on Shalom farm. We have been to Israel and to Tabgha, the place where the historians will tell you that Jesus multiplied the fish and bread to feed five thousand men. The place had a tremendous impact on me, but nothing like what happened at the Mighty Men™ Conference on Shalom.

> That same miracle took place here on Shalom farm.

I remember a gentleman, William O'Brian, who had come up to the conference from Pinetown. He wanted to spend time with God. I remember seeing him sitting in the grass with his Bible on his lap. He had pitched his one-man tent right next to his pick-up. He was completely at peace, just enjoying his heavenly Father's creation. That night, William had a huge heart attack and went home to be with Jesus. I struggled to sleep that night and asked the Lord, "What's going on here, Lord?" I realized that people die, and the larger the crowd of men, the greater the chance of someone dying. The death of William O'Brian caused a tremendous sense of urgency in the camp. On the Sunday morning a great number of people made first-time commitments to the Lord and many people made recommitments, too. Men realized that they needed to get their lives ready for the call of the Lord, as it could happen to anyone at any time.

This was also the year that the movie *Faith like Potatoes* was made. The cast, actors, film crew, and producers came onto the stage and received a rousing applause. The movie is still being watched around the world, especially in the USA. Just the other day, I received the latest translation of the book by the same name, but in Italian. God works through very ordinary people. That little book has been translated into about fifteen or sixteen different languages. The conference ended with a mighty wind, which split the food tent in half, from top to bottom. This tent was situated next to the five thousand-seater tent. The intercessors interpreted this to be a sign that God was doing a very special work among the men.

Of one thing I am convinced: the Holy Spirit is a God of order, but He won't be put in a box. He will do whatever He sees fit; if He decides to cause a riot first in order to bring about Revival that is what He will do. If God wants to split a tent in half to make a point, that's what He will do.

I have had some criticism about the En-Gedi event; some say that God is a God of order. I received one email that said God would never blow the Holy Bible off the pulpit like He did to my Bible. I have studied Revival since it is my favourite subject and later on we will take a closer look at some of them. I have seen time and again how God will do whatever He needs to, to get our attention.

In the Hebrides Revival, God shook a stone house, and the dishes and cutlery rattled on the shelves. This got the whole village out onto the street so that God could speak to them.

The same thing happened in the southern part of Africa, in a small town called Worcester. A mighty wind blew through a church while young people were having a youth meeting. This caught the attention of the young people and they went out and set South Africa on fire. I love God with an absolute reverent passion; however, I will never limit God.

The following Mighty Men™ Conference, we trusted God for twenty-three thousand men. That number had been shouted out by a man who attended the Mighty

Men™ Conference the year before. I spent time with the Lord and felt that Father wanted me to book the biggest tent in the world.

I contacted my producer of *Grassroots*, George Carpenter. I asked him to find out online where the biggest tent in the world could be found. He phoned me back and said that, believe it or not, it was situated in Johannesburg, South Africa. It had been built in the UK, was extended in Europe, and was now housed in Johannesburg. It had only ever been erected three times, and had never before been erected in the countryside.

We inquired about hiring the tent and found that it would cost millions of rands. We went ahead and booked it by faith, in 2008. Something like sixteen to eighteen heavy-duty trucks came rolling into the farm with the huge tent on board. The excitement was electrifying. It took two to three weeks to erect the tent with professional riggers (no farmers were allowed to touch the tent!). Diesel-powered generators were needed to pull the centre masts up into place; it sure was something to see.

> It took two to three weeks to erect the tent with professional riggers.

Attie van Staden was the tent master and it was the biggest tent he had ever erected. It was an unbelievable structure to see once it was in place, and even had its own weather station on site as the weather needed to be monitored day and night. The steel cables that held it up needed to be constantly tensioned depending on the wind velocity.

The tent covered an area equivalent to three football fields. We hired thirty thousand chairs, which Dougal Maclean, my son-in-law, positioned for us inside the tent. Another thirty thousand men were seated outside. The open sides of the tent stood about 9 metres high, with the stage right in the centre.

My oldest son, Andy, was heading up the praise and worship. He, together with Clive Tedder, was my right-hand man in organizing the conference. They said that the speakers we had would not supply sufficient sound to the tent – the experts can determine to the very row of chairs how far the sound will reach.

I told Andy that our budget was already stretched to the limit and we could not afford to spend more on a sound system. Andy was adamant and said that if the men could not hear the Gospel being preached, what was the point? He was quite right. So, by raw faith, we ordered more speakers that cost us around R250,000. I watched as a truckload of speakers arrived at the farm and my faith was really tested.

At the same time, God was speaking to a stock farmer in the Free State. That farmer sold four hundred prime quality sheep and anonymously put the money into our account. That money arrived the day after we had agreed to the added cost of more speakers. This occurred not before, but straight after we had decided to trust God.

We expected twenty-three thousand men and about sixty thousand men arrived. The men stayed for the entire weekend and we managed to feed them all. It was a most incredible happening. That was the last time we were able to feed this huge multitude of men – the numbers were getting out of hand!

After the 2008 Mighty Men™ Conference, the Lord challenged me not to count numbers anymore. I was reminded of what happened to King David in the Old Testament when he insisted on taking a census of all the fighting men in Israel. The Lord was displeased with David and punished him severely by killing something like seventy thousand people, who died of the plague.

I asked the Lord to show me why He was so displeased by the census. The Master showed me this: when David was a young shepherd boy, he trusted in God alone to fight his battles; first against lions and bears and then later against Goliath. But once David was established by God as the greatest king Israel had ever had, he put his trust in the might, strength, and number of his own fighting force and not in God.

After the 2008 Mighty Men™ Conference, we decided to go open air; there was no tent big enough to host the vast crowds of men. We need to remember that it was only *men* attending, not women and children. When we look at the average church meeting on a Sunday, the congregation mostly comprises women and children, with a few men dotted throughout.

This is what makes the move of God amongst the men so miraculous. We thank God for faithful women and children. Things have changed in South Africa; we are seeing churches filled with men and this is truly God's heart. There were so many miracles that took place during the "Big Tent" gathering in 2008, but I cannot mention them all.

> Things have changed in South Africa; we are seeing churches filled with men and this is truly God's heart.

One incident I remember clearly occurred on the Saturday night. While preaching, I said to the men, "Tomorrow morning we need to get up early. We need to get packed, because after the final service it is going to rain."

It had not rained the whole weekend. The service on Sunday finished at around eleven o'clock. As we left the big tent, huge drops of rain started to fall. Just as the last vehicles left the farm, the heavens opened up and it poured endlessly for three days and three nights. It washed the farm clean.

After the conference, some men came down from Johannesburg and offered to buy the big tent for the ministry at Shalom. We thanked them, but I needed clear confirmation from God first. After waiting on the Lord about the matter, I felt God tell me to decline the offer. Reluctantly, we told the men our decision and thanked them for their kind offer. In hindsight I realize it was the right decision – that tent took 1 million rand to erect each time. We would have needed a fleet of 30-

ton trucks to transport it to the venue.

What happened in 2009 no tent in the world would have been able to facilitate. When the time for the 2009 Mighty Men™ Conference arrived, we erected a stage right in the middle of the farm. It was open-air and we positioned hay bales and chairs around the stage in the form of a cartwheel. So when I preached, I walked around in circles. The men arrived in their thousands and the sound system was absolutely amazing. It flowed out over all the fields we had reserved for the conference. The day/night screens that you see at large sporting events were positioned every hundred metres; nothing was spared or left to chance.

Men arrived from the four corners of the earth; from Australia, Pakistan, Zimbabwe, Israel, Britain, and from many other places. The first night arrived; the platform was the height of a house. Beneath the stage we had hung shade cloth. The music team sat in this area while I was preaching. It was extremely warm in this area as the shade cloth did not allow for air circulation.

The response on Friday night was electric and masses of men stood for Christ. On Saturday morning I spoke for an hour and it was very hot. I went down under the stage at the end of the sermon and Andy and the music team continued to play music while the men walked back to their campsites.

I had made an appointment to meet farmers from Australia, who had come from every state: the Northern Territory, Queensland, New South Wales, Western Australia, and even Tasmania. They were waiting for me under the stage. I started to pray for them individually, over thirty-five farmers. I prophesied over them too.

At the end of my prayers, I began to feel very weak and lightheaded. I walked towards the exit to get some fresh air, but collapsed. At that moment, Andy had finished singing and was walking down the stairs. He caught me as I fell. When I regained consciousness, I had no idea where I was. I thought it might just be excessive fatigue that had caused me to collapse. In fact I had just had my first heart attack.

The paramedics gave me oxygen, put me in a car, and drove me to my house about a kilometre away. I sat in the garden quietly and Jill gave me a sweet cup of tea. I thought everything would be fine. I drank half the cup of tea and collapsed again.

This time I stayed down. My blood pressure was at zero and the paramedics were struggling to keep me alive. Pure adrenaline was injected into my body; something that is usually done as a last resort.

A helicopter arrived from Durban to transport me to Pietermaritzburg. The helicopter was piloted by a woman, who flew fast and with great skill. The helicopter landed next to my house, and the paramedics cut the fence and came through the garden with a stretcher. I could hear everything and see everything, but I couldn't speak. I was saying in my heart, *Lord Jesus, what is going on? I don't understand: this is the finest time of my life and the wheels are coming off. This is an absolute disaster!* And yet I was at peace about the whole incident.

We had about forty aeroplanes parked at a nearby airstrip, together with nine helicopters. None of them were rigged out to deal with heart attacks. That is why a 911 helicopter had been called. A patient needs to lie flat after having a seizure. I was strapped to a stretcher and carried to the helicopter. The paramedics were Christians and were praying for me.

As we took off, the pilot swooped over the vast crowd of men. By this time Andy had called the men back to the stage area and they were fervently praying for me. I had a sideways glimpse out of the helicopter and saw a sight I shall never forget: thousands upon thousands of men had their hands stretched to the sky praying for my recovery. God is so good. We got to Pietermaritzburg in fifteen minutes and when the helicopter touched down at the hospital helipad, I was totally healed.

The cardiologist, a wonderful Muslim doctor, made me run on a treadmill for a good few minutes with wires attached to my body. After looking at the screen in front of him, he said, "Mr Buchan, I have something to tell you. There is nothing wrong with your heart; you may go home." I was healed! I did feel washed out, however, like I had been hit by a big Mack Truck.

The incident changed the whole spirit at the conference. Men were weeping openly, everywhere. Not for me, but for themselves, for their families, and for the nation. Many men told me afterwards that the Saturday night meeting when I had been absent was the best meeting of all (nothing like keeping a man humble!).

There was a wonderful spirit of reconciliation that took place, so much love – godly love – among the men.

The Lord gave me clear instruction to stage one more Mighty Men™ Conference in 2010. We had the biggest crowd of all the conferences and arranged five entrances into the farm but there were still traffic jams everywhere. While travelling to the conference, men would stop at road-houses en route, and shout "AMEN" (which had become a Mighty Men™ Conference war cry), and many of the men would respond with an "AMEN" back. It was an unbelievable time.

We were told that an aeroplane was taking off from the airport in Durban, bound for Cape Town. The captain taxied to the top of the runway and turned for take off, but stopped the plane and said over the intercom, "Gentlemen, could we pray together before we take off?" The plane was full, jam-packed with big, strong men. The airline had sent the men's luggage on a different plane because of the weight factor. Hearing the men pray along with the pilot before flying back to Cape Town must have warmed the Father's heart. A tremendous spirit of oneness was formed during this Revival.

The 2010 Mighty Men™ Conference was structured in a different way, in Zulu style. Traditionally, Zulu impi would fight in the shape of a bull's horns. They would have the main force in the centre and the younger men on the two flanks. We built a huge platform on the lowest part of the farm, like a natural amphitheatre. The seats were spread up the middle and then to both sides. We used acres and acres of farmland.

There was no guarantee that anyone was going to arrive; the whole event takes place by raw faith. No specific church group or denomination backs us. That's why I go up the mountain and spend time in blood, sweat, and tears. The team are so busy organizing the event that they do not have the time to consider the dire consequences if everything fails.

I spend time on a mountain overlooking the farm, in a pine plantation. The devil tells me that the men will not come back and I am going to go under. The Holy Spirit asks me a question, "Have We ever let you down before?" The bottom line is that unless God sends the men, no one will come. (I have the smallest understanding of what Jesus must have felt like at Gethsemane.)

Gethsemane means "olive press", a very fitting name when we think of what our Lord and Saviour went through for you and me. I sat on top of that mountain and cried out to God, "Please, send the men."

On the Wednesday before the meetings were due to start, I heard a rumble in the distance, like the "sound of marching in the tops of the mulberry trees" (1 Chronicles 14:15). My spirit leapt within me; it was the sound of vehicles coming from the north, south, east, and west. Columns of dust rose and the men started to arrive. I was sitting on the high place so I could see it unfolding before me. I saw caravans, bikes, pick-ups, and trucks; they were all on their way to meet with the living God. It was as chaotic as a metropolitan city!

The men in charge of traffic control were fully stretched. There was a wonderful atmosphere; despite the traffic and excitement there was an amazing spirit of peace in the campsites. A large contingent of policemen on the farm monitored everything – there were actually more men at the farm than comprised the entire South African defence force. There was not one incident of unrest for the duration of the conference. The policemen themselves enjoyed the weekend immensely; I trust that many of them had their lives changed for the better through the power of the Holy Spirit.

It is a total mystery to me why Father God chooses to use doubters like myself to do His work. One minute I was crying out to Jesus to please send the men, and then I was crying out to God to please keep them there. If men do not like what they hear, they simply pack up camp and head home.

> I stood on the platform on the first evening, so proud to be a child of God, knowing full well that our Lord Holy Spirit was standing right next to me.

There was a real cross-section of society: drug addicts, men from broken homes, men from huge organizations and mining houses as well as country boys, professional sportsmen, and school teachers. Fully responsible young men of twelve years of age also attended. There was a great spirit of "fathers and sons" at the conference.

I stood on the platform on the first evening, so proud to be a child of God, knowing full well that our Lord

Holy Spirit was standing right next to me.

I can say, like Robert Murray McCheyne (who started a Revival in Dundee, Scotland, many years ago), "Rather than having been an instrument of the Lord, all I was was an adoring spectator."

Hearts were broken; men were set free and many found a new hope and vision. We shouted our war cry together as God's army: "AMEN" (which means "so be it") and the sound thundered through the vast sea of men. We were told later that the Mighty Men™ war cry could be heard from 15 kilometres away. The weekend came to a close on the Sunday morning, when the women and children joined us.

> I felt God tell me that this would be the last MMC, one of the hardest decisions I have had to make in my life – and yet it never was mine in the first place.

I felt God tell me that this would be the last Mighty Men™ Conference, one of the hardest decisions I have had to make in my life – and yet it never was mine in the first place. Men came to me from far and wide and asked if I knew what I was doing. Respectable men came to me and asked me to carefully reconsider my decision. They suggested that this move of God needed to be nurtured and put into order and even formed into an organization! My response was that we cannot contain the move of God; we cannot put our Creator in a box any more than we can harness the wind. God started it and He would continue it.

I commissioned all the men to take up the baton and to continue the Holy Spirit fire that began in 2003. That is exactly what has happened. There are Mighty Men™ Conferences in the Karoo and in the Eastern Cape, which thousands of men attend. There are other campaigns in Paarl in the Cape and up in the northern part of South Africa in Polokwane, where multitudes of men attend the event year after year. Men are meeting in Australia and Tasmania and the UK.

In 2012 I was in Yorkshire, in Pateley Bridge, at a meeting organized by one of my spiritual sons, Ian Gray. Again Father God ministered wonderfully and deeply to those tough Yorkshire men. We met in Worcestershire at "Top Barn Farm", where David Harper has been doing outstanding work with the men in the Midlands for years. The tent was overflowing for each meeting. There are many other groups meeting together all over the world. It is so exciting to get these reports and there are many I am not even aware of. It confirms to me that this is a work of God and not of man.

Movements have also been born out of the Mighty Men™ Conference events, like "Manne van die Woord". Places like Namibia, Swaziland, the Kalahari, and the Vaal Dam are all having Men's Christian meetings.

I returned recently from Nashville, Tennessee, in the USA. The organizers were expecting two and a half thousand people to turn up and over four thousand men arrived. They have asked me to return this year and are expecting sixteen thousand men in an indoor basketball stadium.

There have been "Mighty Dads and Sons" meetings, "Mighty Music Festivals", and "Mighty Children's Conferences" taking place, which I have had nothing to do with. I simply thank God for them.

The fruit of Revival has got to bring change to the community and to the nation; otherwise it is just another event. The letters and testimonies that we have received are so encouraging. We also received a letter saying that there had been great changes in the mines. Mining is an extremely taxing way to make a living and very hard on these men and their families. The letter said that the miners coming up from underground were praying for the next shift about to go down and that the pubs and canteens at the mines were closing.

Men have gone into full-time ministry as a result of the Mighty Men™ Conferences. Men have reconsidered taking their own lives after meeting with Jesus at a Mighty Men™ Conference. Others have gone home and asked their wives and children for forgiveness and have started a brand-new life in Christ – surely that is Revival.

A few years ago, a very distinguished man, F. C. Hamman, came to see me on my farm. He is an international filmmaker. He was extremely emotional as we sat down together in my office. He told me that he didn't want money or anything from me; he didn't want fame or recognition – he had all that. He said, "I want to do something special for God."

He told me he wanted to make a film about men whose lives had been changed through the Mighty Men™ Conferences. That was the birth of the film called *Angus Buchan's Ordinary People*. It is about three different accounts of men who came to the 2010 Mighty Men™ Conference.

The first story is about two Afrikaans men driving up from the Cape to Shalom. En route the driver is hijacked by a young black man called Lucky Nzimande. He manages to overpower Lucky and handcuffs him to the inside of his pick-up while he decides what to do. Lucky ends up at the event, where he is gloriously saved. After his conversion he went back to a huge squatter township on the outskirts of Cape Town, where he is now preaching the Gospel of Jesus Christ – another evangelist for God.

The second story is about a man who came to the Mighty Men™ Conference because his life was in a mess and the situation was almost beyond repair. On the Saturday evening, under the stars, God touched his life. He phoned his wife and told her to get the family together because he was coming home. Early the next morning he headed home, not even staying for the Sunday morning service. He got on his huge lime-green road bike and left the farm, but he never reached home – he had an accident and was killed. Yet through the tragic accident, his family were brought much closer together, and more importantly, closer to Jesus. John 12:24 says that, "Unless a grain of wheat falls into the ground and dies, it remains

> Through the tragic accident, his family were brought much closer together, and more importantly, closer to Jesus.

alone; but if it dies, it produces much grain." This man's death changed his family and through the movie has touched multitudes all over the world.

The third story is about a father and his son who could just not get on. They could not see eye to eye on anything. The more Dad bought "things" for his boy, the farther they drifted apart. The young man got involved with alcohol and drugs. In a desperate state, the son goes to a Mighty Men™ Conference; he is radically saved and delivered. Father and son are now serving the Lord with all their hearts.

We have a serious problem in the world at present: there are very few spiritual fathers

The key to Revival is to only do what Jesus tells you to do. A good idea is not necessarily a God idea, and a need does not justify a call. When Jesus walked on earth, He did not feed all the hungry and He did not heal all the sick. Jesus only did what His Father told Him to do. We, too, need to be obedient to what the Holy Spirit instructs us to do – no more and no less.

I shudder to think what would have happened if I had not followed God's instructions and continued with my own preaching itinerary. God would have used somebody else and I would have missed out on one of the most blessed experiences of my life.

Do what the Holy Spirit tells you to do and not what people tell you. Get Christians to confirm the Word God has given you; get those who are willing to help involved. If God has given you the vision, then He will supply the finance and every other aspect of the campaign. God is no man's debtor. He works for Himself, not for men. He is God: He is the Alpha and the Omega, the Beginning and the End.

The ingredients for Revival are faith, prayer, and lots of blood, sweat, and tears. Second Chronicles 7:14 says, "If My people who are called by My name will humble themselves, and pray and seek My face, and turn from their wicked ways, then I will hear from heaven, and will forgive their sin and heal their land."

> The ingredients for Revival are faith, prayer, and lots of blood, sweat, and tears.

For men to see genuine Revival there has to be *repentance*, otherwise there can be no Revival. If people are not prepared to say sorry and change, to humble themselves before Almighty God, then Revival cannot manifest itself.

Revival happened at the Mighty Men™ Conferences. There was reconciliation between black and white, between male and female, and between young and old. This only happens when God intervenes. He is the only One who can bring a spirit of forgiveness, healing, and renewal.

At the moment my heart is very heavy for the USA. I have never had a desire in the past to go there and yet God sent me in 2012. The response I received was so precious. The people there gave me a three-minute standing ovation when I got onto the platform. I didn't know what to do. They were loving, gracious, humble men who are looking for father figures. We born-again,

Spirit-filled men need to be fathers to the fatherless.

In James 1:27 Jesus says that pure religion is this: "to visit orphans and widows in their trouble, and to keep oneself unspotted from the world." As I travel around the world, I see that people are seeking the truth and the way. They will try anything to find the true answer to life.

Believers cannot continue to be bystanders and spectators. We have to get into the fight. There is such a need. Ministers cannot do it all as they are busy shepherding their own flocks. God uses nobodies like you and me to do His bidding. People are open to hearing the gospel of Jesus Christ like never before. We need to roll up our sleeves and get to work.

I have had lots of exciting things happen in my life: being a cowboy and riding horses for a living, picking pineapples, working as a coal heaver, and stacking bricks from a kiln. I started farming twice over from nothing and built up to a business with a 20-ton Mercedes Benz with a sound system and lighting plant to take the gospel to Africa.

God has blessed me with many experiences, but nothing can compare with seeing a life changed in the twinkling of an eye. I have letters in a file that have been written by young children of around ten and eleven years, saying, "Thank you, Uncle Angus. I had a brand-new Daddy come home from the Mighty Men™ Conference."

I have letters from women saying, "The man I fell in love with twenty years ago came back after the weekend spent at the Mighty Men™ Conference. Thank you." I have letters from farmers who are now starting their work day with prayer and a Scripture reading and the singing of hymns, changing the whole atmosphere at work.

Men have come of age, and have met with the living God in a natural and spectacular way. I have photographs of miracles taking place. I was sent a photo of a cloud that had a heart shape cut through the middle of it. This cloud was positioned above the thousands of campers, as if Father God was saying, "Boys, I'm pleased with you."

If we want to continue seeing God move we need to believe and expect. I am a farmer with my feet firmly planted on the ground and one thing I have learned is that my Lord is real and He is alive and He is the same yesterday, today, and forever.

After what happened at En-Gedi, I will never be the same again and I shall never limit God. The race is not over; the best is yet to come. In these last days we are going to witness events that have never been seen before. Acts 2:17–21 says:

> And it shall come to pass in the last days, says God, that I will pour out of My Spirit on all flesh; your sons and your daughters shall prophesy, your young men shall see visions, your old men shall dream dreams. And on My menservants and on My maidservants I will pour out My Spirit in those days; and they shall prophesy. I will show wonders in Heaven above and signs in the earth beneath: Blood and fire and vapor of smoke. The sun shall be turned into darkness,

and the moon into blood, before the coming of the great
and notable day of the Lord. And it shall come to pass that
whoever calls upon the name of the Lord shall be saved.

I believe we are in that time now and that is why there
is such a mighty harvest waiting to be reaped. God is no
respecter of persons; if you put your hand up, He will
use you. We need to be obedient and do exactly what
the Father tells us to do.

Signs and wonders are going to become more and
more the order of the day. The chasm between good and
evil is widening: evil shall become more evil and the
righteous more righteous.

I really enjoy spending time with young people; they
have soft hearts and are teachable. They are ready to
receive what God has for them. We need to be available,
prepared, and ready, because the coming of the Lord is
going to happen, and I can't wait!

Revivals of the Past

ELEVEN

The Andrew Murray Revival: 1860

J C de Vries was the youth leader at a church in Worcester, Western Cape. He later became the minister of the Dutch Reformed Church. He left us with the following eye witness account:

> On a certain Sunday evening there were gathered in a little hall some sixty young people. I was leader of the meeting, which commenced with a hymn and a lesson from God's Word after which I engaged in prayer. After three or four others had (as was customary) given out a verse and offered prayer, a coloured girl of about fifteen years of age, in the service of a farmer from Hex River, rose at the back of the hall and asked if she might propose a hymn.
>
> At first I hesitated, not knowing what the meeting would think, but better thoughts prevailed and I replied, "Yes." She

gave out her hymn verse and prayed out in moving tones. While she was praying we heard a sound in the distance which came nearer and nearer, until the hall seemed to be shaken and with one or two exceptions the whole meeting began to pray – the majority in audible voice, but some in whispers. Nevertheless, the noise made by the concourse was deafening. A feeling which I cannot describe took possession of me.

Even now forty-three years after the occurrences, the events of that never to be forgotten night passed before my mind's eye like a soul-stirring panorama. I feel again as I then felt, and cannot refrain from pushing my chair backwards and thanking the Lord fervently for His mighty deeds.

At that time, Reverend Murray was a minister at Worcester. He had preached that evening in the English language. When the service was over, an elder, Mr Jan Rabie, passed the door of the hall, heard the noise, peeked in and then hastened to call Mr Murray, returning with him. Mr Murray came forward to the table where I knelt praying, touched me and made me understand that he wanted me to rise. He then asked me what had happened. I related everything to him. He then walked down the hall some distance and called out, as loudly as he could, "People, silence!" But the praying continued.

In the meantime I too kneeled down again. It seemed to me that if the Lord was coming to bless us, I should be on my knees not standing. Mr Murray then called again saying, "People I am your minister sent from God, silence!" But there was no stopping the noise. No-one heard him, but all continued praying and calling on God for mercy and pardon. Mr Murray then returned to me and told me to start the

hymn verse commencing ("Aid the Soul that helpless cries").
I did so, but the emotions were not quieted and the meeting
went on praying. Mr Murray then prepared to depart, saying
"God is a God of order and here everything is confusion."
With that he left the hall.

One is left to shake one's head in wonderment at how
Andrew Murray could have turned his back on God's
presence and stalked out of the hall. But having been an eye
witness to the disorderly manifestations at the farm 'Doorns',
(and probably other farms as well) and then experiencing
a similar occurrence with the young people, he must have
dismissed the rowdy praying as an emotional mimicry of
what was taking place on the farms.

For him being godly equated with being orderly.
Furthermore, Andrew's knowledge of Revivals to that point
had been based on the Scottish experience where the
blessing had flowed from the anointed preaching of His
Word. So it is understandable
that He would have questioned
whether the Worcester
experience – where the Holy
Spirit had come in power
without the aid of any agent –
was truly of God. In addition to
this was the fact that the way
God chose to show up did not
fall in his comfort zone.

> Isn't it amazing how
> in Revivals, the very
> men who have been
> fasting and praying for
> Revival do not always
> recognize it, or feel
> comfortable with it,
> when it comes?

Isn't it amazing how in Revivals, the very men who
have been fasting and praying for Revival do not always
recognize it, or feel comfortable with it, when it comes?

Andrew Murray came from a very conservative Scottish background and was uneasy with the so-called unruliness and wild behaviour of the young people. These young people had been totally shattered by the rushing mighty wind that had blown through the "Sending Kerk".

I have been to that church in Worcester and sadly it is no longer a church but has been turned into a café. It is called the Pardon Café, a very appropriate name, and is run by lovely folk.

The proprietors allowed me to go into the back of the building where the original church was. I was deeply touched as I looked up at the rafters and roof structure where the mighty rushing wind would have blown.

We must never try to limit God in the way in which He moves. His ways are not our ways and His thoughts are not our thoughts (see Isaiah 55:8–9).

We continue with De Vries's report:

After that (the outbreak of Revival amongst the young people) the prayer meetings were held every evening. At the commencement there was generally great silence, but after the second or third prayer the whole hall was moved as before and the whole hall was moved to praying. Sometimes these prayer meetings continued to as late as 3 a.m. in the morning, even then many wished to remain longer, or went home singing through the streets. The little hall was soon too small, and the folk were compelled to move to the school building which was also presently full to overflowing, and hundreds of country folk streamed into the village.

On the first Saturday evening in the larger meeting house, Mr Murray was the leader. He read a portion of Scripture, made a few observations, engaged in prayer, then gave others opportunity to pray. During the prayer which followed on his, I heard again the sound in the distance. It drew nearer and nearer, and suddenly the whole gathering was praying. That evening a stranger had been standing at the door from the commencement, watching the proceedings.

Mr Murray descended from the platform and moved up and down among the people, trying to quieten them. The stranger then tiptoed forward from his position at the door to Mr Murray and said to him, be careful what you do here, for it is the Spirit of God at work here. I have just come from America and this is precisely what I witnessed there.

Andrew must have taken the comments of this English stranger to heart, as there is no other record of him trying to ever stop or interfere with the numerous prayer meetings that followed.

The following letter, written by Emma to her mother, mentions the intense excitement that caused some to faint as well as the spiritual wrestling and agony that many had to go through:

We are having many visitors coming to see us from the surrounding places who come to see us on account of the Revival meetings, and go away blessed saying half has never been told. It is a solemn thing to live in such a congregation at such a time. I feel sure the Lord is going to bless us even more, yet there are many heavy trials before us. The work is deeply interesting and yet some things are painful.

In the midst of an earnest address a man drove a dog into the church with a tin tied to its tail and frightened the people. Andrew came down the aisle and prayed a most solemn prayer, that if the work of God was not of God, He Himself would put a stop to it.

The people were terrified, as the excitement was very intense, some even fainted. The prayer meeting last night was very full, and then men decided for Christ, but fifty undecided left the building at twelve midnight. We had no idea of the time.

Two souls came through afterwards who were wrestling in agony for a time but got into the light in their own houses. Some go through a fiery struggle! Two sisters have passed through and are now bright and rejoicing.

Last night again the church was full and Andrew preached so powerfully and yet so simply on the Lamb of God. He is so very discreet in dealing with souls. About twenty came forward and others stayed behind to be spoken to. We do feel and realise the power and presence of God so mightily. His Spirit is indeed being poured out among us.

There is another account written by Hessie Bosman, who had come to stay with De Vries. She was a teacher but was in poor health. He advised her not to attend the meetings, but she felt she should attend. This is how the letter was written:

She said she had to go, even if it should prove her death. She had prayed so much for these meetings that she felt she could not stay away, come what may I am going, she said. She attended and was the third to engage in prayer that evening.

While praying the whole meeting broke out into prayer while she fell unconscious to the floor. I carried her to the parsonage, De Vries said, where they were some time in bringing her around. That night she had to remain at the parsonage and the next day she was fully recovered.

This is an account of Andrew Murray senior, who visited the place to see first-hand what God was doing through the Revival. He had been praying faithfully for thirty-eight years for his own congregation at Graaff-Reinet to be awakened. It must have been a bitter-sweet experience for him to witness the power of God moving through the Worcester congregation, while as yet there was no stirring of any dry bones in Graaff-Reinet. Nevertheless, he blessed God for the opportunity to be present and to address the Revival meeting. He is recorded as saying:

Andrew, my son, I have longed for times as these which the Lord has let you have.

This awakening spread through Worcester, Tulbach, Ceres, Paarl, and then moved up into the Eastern Cape into towns like Graaff-Reinet, Aberdeen, Somerset East, Adelaide, Queenstown, Sterkstroom, and Lady Grey. It continued up into the Free State, to Bloemfontein, Harrismith, Ladysmith, then on into Durban, KwaZulu-Natal, and through the nation.

Andrew Murray gives his final word on this awakening. He says:

> In conclusion, I ask permission to give one word of advice to my reader. It is this. It needs time to grow into Jesus the Vine. Do not expect to abide in Him unless you give Him that time. It is not enough to read God's Word or meditate, and then think that we have hold of the thoughts and have asked God for His blessing, to go out and hope that the blessing will abide. No, it needs day by day, time with Jesus and with God!

I personally had the privilege of preaching outside that beautiful mother church in Worcester at the one hundred and fiftieth anniversary of the Andrew Murray Revival. A huge Coca-Cola flat-bed truck was parked on the street in front of the church and the crowd was seated on parkland across the road.

The Gospel of Jesus Christ was preached and an altar call made. Those wanting to make a stand for Christ were asked to walk past the truck and into the magnificent church, and in a reverent attitude of prayer, make a confession to Christ together. The mother church was full of repentant souls, weeping and making first-time commitments to Christ, with others making recommitments.

TWELVE

The Hebrides Revival: 1949

I received a little book by Duncan Campbell about the Hebrides Revival from our intercessor Peggy O' Neil.

Peggy was a prayer warrior, someone who prayed tirelessly for me and for the work we are doing at Shalom. She is with our Father now, and she will be smiling down at me for writing a book about the "rushing mighty wind" of the Holy Spirit.

I have studied Revivals for many years, but this particular book has changed my life. In the introduction it says that our God is a covenant-keeping God and that He will always honour His side of an agreement.

The Hebrides Revival took place on the isles of Lewis and Harris, on the north-west coast of bonnie Scotland. Duncan Campbell was invited to hold an evangelical outreach. The inhabitants of these little islands on the coast of Scotland had been praying for years for a spiritual awakening. Two elderly sisters (one was blind and the other crippled with arthritis) had been praying unceasingly for God to send a "rushing, mighty wind".

Campbell arrived on a small fishing boat. He was met by clergymen and the two Morris sisters. One of the sisters said, "Mr Campbell, do you know God?" Campbell was quite taken aback by the question. "I really do hope so," he replied.

However, Campbell was met with resistance on the islands. Resistance is not uncommon – we sometimes have a concept of how Revival will come, but Jesus doesn't do things the way we want, but rather in obedience to His heavenly Father.

God will not be dictated to by any church or organization, because He is God. Our Father sends His Holy Spirit when He sees fit, which might not be convenient for us or for the church. God has a habit of using "ordinary people" to do His bidding. Campbell faced tremendous criticism from the local church; only seven people came to his meetings.

At the close of one meeting, the missions clerk of the church in which Duncan was ministering, said, "These go not out but by prayer and fasting." So they met in a local farmhouse down the road and spent the night in prayer. Campbell wrote:

So we met. There were about thirty of us, and prayer began. I found it a very hard meeting. I found myself battling and getting nowhere as the hours passed. After midnight between 12 midnight and one in the morning, I turned to a young man in the meeting and felt prompted to ask Him to pray.

That dear young man rose to his feet and prayed and in his prayer he uttered words such as I have never heard in a prayer meeting before. He said, "Lord, You made a promise, are You going to fulfill it? We believe that You are a covenant-keeping God, will You be true to Your covenant? You have said that You will pour out water on the thirsty and floods upon the dry ground. I do not know how others stand in Your presence, I do not know how the ministers stand, but if I know my own heart, I know where I stand and I tell You now that I am thirsty, O, I am thirsty for a manifestation of the Man of Your right hand," and then he said this, "Lord, before I sit down I want to tell You that Your honour is at stake."

You cannot pray a prayer like that if you are not walking closely with God. Have you ever prayed a prayer like that? That young man prayed a prayer of faith.

I like to think that the angels and archangels look over the battlements of glory and say to one another, "This is a man who believes in God. This is a man who dares to stand firm on the promise of God and takes from the throne what the throne has promised!"

The house shook like a leaf, the dishes rattled on the sideboard and an elder standing beside me said, "Mr Campbell, an earth tremor." I said, "Yes!" and pronounced the benediction immediately, and we walked out of the house to find the community alive with an awareness of God.

Men and women were carrying stools and chairs and asking, "Is there room for us in the church?" The Revival did not break out because Duncan Campbell was there. No, a thousand times, no, but because God found a man He could trust, a man who dared to believe the promise of God.

I hear men saying at meetings, "Lord, I am claiming Revival, claiming Revival." We ought to be careful what we say. If we claim it, we have it; yes, this is a glorious possibility. Indeed I would go so far as to say, if I did not believe this I would go back to business. And I believe that when God finds clean hands, and pure hearts, we shall find springs in the desert, and rivers in the dry places.

Seven American ministers were on the Isle of Lewis some time ago. They were walking through a certain valley when they heard singing coming from this direction and coming from that direction and this is what was being sung:

"His name forever shall endure;
Last like the sun it shall:
Men shall be blessed in Him, and blessed,
All nations shall Him call.
And blessed be the Lord our God,
The God of Israel.
For He alone doth wondrous works in glory
that excel.
And blessed be His glorious name.
To all eternity;
The whole earth let His glory fill,
Amen, so let it be."

One of the ministers turned to the others and said, "This is Heaven, Heaven around us." The parish will never forget that night. Revival blessing had come, and now it had reached flood tide. That night some of the men and women on the crest of its wave were swept into the Kingdom of God. O that God would do it again.

My dear people, let us get on our faces before God and pray that He may yet visit us in mercy and that we, His people, may yet once again ascend the hill of God and stand in His holy place. May God grant it.

> What amazes me is that every Revival or awakening that God brings about has certain elements that are common. The main one is repentance.

What amazes me is that every Revival or awakening that God brings about has certain elements that are common. The main one is repentance. People are always called to repent, to change from their wicked ways.

People are driven to prayer, and then driven to worship God in Spirit and in truth. The young man's prayer was bold and sincere, from the heart.

I believe God heard that prayer just like He heard the prayer of Moses. God was about to destroy the nation of Israel. He had had enough of His people's pride, their arrogance and stiff-necked attitude.

But Moses said to God that He could not do it, because the other nations would mock God. God relented and the children of Israel were saved. When God sees the authentic hearts of His people, He sends Revival.

I love John Wesley's definition of Revival: "A people saturated by God".

Campbell relates the following:

I could take you to a little cottage in the Hebrides and introduce you to a young woman. She is not educated; she was not polished in the sense that we use the word, but I have known that young woman to pray heaven into a community, to pray power into a meeting. I have known that woman to be caught up in the power of the Holy Spirit that men and women around her were made to tremble – not influence, but power.

The apostles were not men of influence, "not many mighty, not many great". Oh no, the Master Himself did not choose to be a man of influence. "He made Himself a man of no reputation", all of which is equal of saying that God chose power over influence.

Oh, that the Church today, in our congregations, in our pulpits would rediscover this truth, and get back to the place of God-realization, to the place of power. I want to say further that we should seek power, even at the expense of influence. What do I mean by that? I mean this: never compromise to accommodate the devil.

I hear, people say today, these are different days to the days of the 1859 Revival, or the Welsh Revival; we must be tolerant and we must try to accommodate. In order to do that it is sometimes necessary to lower our standard and seek the co-operation of those who do not accept the position we hold relative to evangelical truth.

The secret of power is to be separate from all that which

is unclean, for me there is nothing as unclean as the liberal views held by some today. We dare not touch them. I am stating what to me is a deep-seated conviction: "Come out from among them and be ye separate... and touch not the unclean thing, and I will receive you, and will be a Father unto you."

Campbell continues:

Now the person who will take his stand on that ground will not be popular. He will not be popular with some preachers of today who declare that we must soft-pedal in order to capture and captivate. Here I quote from the saintly Charles Finney, "Away with your milk and water preaching of the love of Christ which has no holiness or moral discrimination in it, away with the preaching of Christ not crucified for sin." Such a collapse of conscience in this land could never have existed if the Puritan element in our preaching had not, in a great measure, fallen out.

Here is the quotation from a Highland minister preaching on this very truth. He cried: "Bring me a God all mercy but not just, bring me a God all love but not righteous, and I will have no scruples in calling Him an idiot of your imagination."

Strong words, but I protest, words that I would sound throughout this land today in this age of desperate apostasy, forsaking all the fundamental truths of Scripture.

Here you have the early apostles proclaiming a message that was profoundly disturbing. We are afraid of disturbing people today. You must not have their emotions stirred, you must not have people weeping in a meeting, you must not have people rolling on the floor under the conviction of sin; keep things orderly.

May God help us, may God have mercy upon us. Who are we to dictate to Almighty God as to how He is going to work?

> **Who are we to dictate to Almighty God as to how He is going to work?**

If God chooses to move in that way, if God chooses to move in that way, if God chooses to so convict men and women of their sin that they will be about to lose their reason, I say, God, move on, until we see again what was witnessed in the Edwards Revival, in the Finney Revival, in the '59 Revival, in the Welsh Revival, and, praise God, today in the Hebrides Revival – God moving in supernatural reality.

Campbell goes on to say:

There are those who say, "But we must not frighten people." I would to God that a real wave of real godly fear would grip our land. Let me quote from a sermon delivered by the Rev. Robert Barr of the Presbyterian Church of South Africa:

> *"This is what our age needs, not an easy-moving message, the sort of thing that makes the hearer feel all nice inside, but rather a message profoundly disturbing.*
>
> *"We have been far too afraid of disturbing people, but the Holy Spirit will have nothing to do with a message or a minister who is afraid of disturbing.*

> "You might as well let a surgeon give place to a quack who claims to be able to do the job with some sweet-tasting drug, as expect the Holy Spirit to agree that the tragic plight of human souls today can be met by soft and easy words.
>
> "Calvary was anything but nice to look at – blood-soaked wood, a bruised and bleeding body – not nice to look upon. But then Jesus was not dealing with a nice thing, He was dealing with the sin of the world, and that is what we are called upon to deal with today. Soft and easy words, soft-pedaling will never meet the need."

My prayer is that Romans 8:19, "For the earnest expectation of the creation eagerly waits for the revealing of the sons of God," will happen again in our beloved nation and in the world, before it is too late.

The world has no answers; we see wars and rumours of wars, destruction, chaos, immorality, and open disrespect and mockery of Jesus Christ. The world knows no better. Creation is waiting to see what we are going to do.

God, please put a fire in our hearts, that we may have sleepless nights, that we may have ongoing prayer until there is Revival, a world Revival. It is the only thing that will save this very sick world of ours.

THIRTEEN

The Indonesian Revival: 1965

*L*ike *A Mighty Wind*, written in 1971, speaks of a Revival that took place on the small island of Timor, Indonesia, in 1965. God used a man by the name of Mel Tari. Tari emphasizes that God's Spirit brings not only power, but also love and discipline.

The book speaks of miracles that took place similar to those in the day of Jesus: water was turned into wine; people were raised from the dead; men walked across a 30-foot-deep, swollen river.

The awakening impacted a network of islands in the Pacific Ocean. The Indonesian Bible Society tried to chart the results but found it impossible to keep up. Churches in central Java, for example, reported thirty thousand members in 1961 and now number about a hundred thousand.

The Revival began in the City of Soe on the island of Timor. A local Methodist minister in Bandung, Reverend

Thomas, said, "These people are very primitive. They have always lived in a spirit world and they readily understand the conflict between good and evil spirits. With their childlike faith, miracles are no problem for them."

Many church leaders believe that we are living on the threshold of the time when the Gospel will move out from Asia to the rest of the world. Tari is one of the men who is going out. Tari was eighteen years old when the Revival started; he is now travelling the world telling his story. He belonged to the Presbyterian Church and said:

I belong to the Presbyterian Church, and we had everything in order. When we went to church, everything was written down on paper. The pastor read one part and we read the other part. We know when to stand, when to sit, when to pray, and when to sing. I really thanked God for, and appreciated, that order in my church. We also had love. Or should I say, we had a little bit of love! When someone smiled at us, we smiled back. We learned to love people if they loved us. And if they didn't love us, we didn't love them too much. But in my church, we had no power at all.

When the Revival came, God gave us all the gifts of the Holy Spirit, as well as power and love and order. I remember well that night of September 26, 1965. About 200 people of all ages were in our church praying together. As we were playing, suddenly something strange took place. If you will read in your Bible, Acts 2, you will find out what happened in my church. We had known this Bible portion for many years.

As a matter of fact, many of us had memorised it, but we had never experienced it in our own lives. Our pastor often said to us, "Since God gave the Holy Spirit to the church 2,000 years ago, if you are a member of the church, automatically you receive the baptism of the Holy Spirit." That night the Lord began to open our eyes that it isn't an automatic thing.

That night as we were praying together, suddenly the Holy Spirit came just as He did on the Day of Pentecost. In Acts 2, we read that He came from heaven like the rushing mighty wind. And that night, as I was sitting next to my sister, I heard this mighty rushing sound. It sounded like a small tornado in the church. I looked around and saw nothing. I turned to my sister. "Dear, do you hear a strange noise?" I asked. "Yes," she replied, "I do. But forget about the sound, and let's pray." She began to pray, and at the same time I heard many others begin to pray. You must know that in our church, we always prayed in absolute order, one by one. For one person to pray in our church was enough, since everything was written out in front of us. If many were to pray, we had to write a whole lot of prayers. But that night those Presbyterians started to forget the written order and the prayers in front of them and began to pray in the Spirit – at first one by one, all before I knew it, they all began to pray at the same time. "Oh, my dear Jesus, what's going on in this church? They have forgotten the written order," I said.

As everyone was praying I looked at the pastors. My, what an anxious look they had on their faces. They were sitting in the front of the church on a platform and they didn't know how to handle those 200 people. They too heard the rushing mighty wind. I looked around again and still there was nothing moving; it was only a sound. Then I heard the fire bell ringing loud and fast. Across the street from the church was the police station and the fire bell. The man in the police station saw that our church was on fire, so he rang the bell to tell the people of the village to come quick, there was a fire! In Indonesia, especially in Timor, we don't have fire trucks. We just ring the bell, and the people realize that there is a fire and come from all over the village with their buckets of water and other things to help put out the fire.

When they got to the church, they saw the flames, but the church wasn't burning. Instead of a natural fire, it was the fire of God. Because of this, many people received Jesus Christ as their Savior and also the baptism of the Holy Spirit. Of course, being Presbyterians, we were not familiar with the words "baptism or infilling of the Holy Spirit." This was something new to us. But the Lord opened our eyes and told us that these are the things we must experience in our lives; that we couldn't depend on the Pentecost of years ago. I thank the Lord that that night He forgave us for our ignorance, and the Holy Spirit moved in a mighty way.

I was sitting near the back of the church, so I was able to see what was going on. Suddenly a sister a little to the front of me stood up and began to raise her hands, "Lord, this sister is breaking the order of our church," I said. "We're not allowed to raise our hands in church." When we went to church, we prayed and put on a holy look. That night, however, that woman stood up and lifted her hands to God! "Lord, what's wrong with this woman?" I said. "This is not to go on in our church. This is not our style." The Lord reminded me that the Bible says, "Lift up your hands in the sanctuary" (Psalm 134:2).

Then I noticed the lady in front of me. She was an illiterate woman and didn't even know our official Indonesian language that is used all over our country. She only spoke her tribal language, which is Timorese. Naturally, she didn't know any English. At that time, however, I knew a little English because I had studied it in school. And this lady began to pray out loud in very beautiful, perfect English, "O, Jesus, I love You," she said, "Oh, I want to take the cross and follow You. Oh, I love You, Jesus," and she just went on and on worshiping the Lord.

My two pastors, who didn't know one single word of English, thought she was gibbering. They ran to the pulpit and cried out, "Oh, Lord, if this is not from You and this is from the devil and the devil has made this gibbering sound, please make them quit." But the more they prayed, the more the Spirit of God poured out His blessing.

Then a man on the other side of the church began to pray in German. He stood there, and the words of praise and worship to the Lord were just beautiful. After that, people began to stand all over the church, worshiping the Lord in different languages. Heaven came down that night, and it was wonderful. Some were speaking in French. Some were praising God in different tribal languages. And one lady just kept saying, "Shalom, Shalom," even though she had no idea she was speaking Hebrew.

When those hundreds of people who came to put out the fire reached the church, they heard the praying and said, "What's going on with these church people? They have never been noisy. They've never prayed much out loud." They crowded into the church to see what was going on, and instead of 200, there were more than 1,000 [people] in our church that night from all over town.

As the Holy Spirit moved, people all over the church came under conviction and accepted Jesus Christ as their own personal Savior. They repented and ran back to their houses and got their witchcraft materials and their fetishes and their astrology stuff and their dirty books and their books on how to interpret dreams and they brought them all back to the church and burned them all in a fire.

No one was preaching that night, but the Holy Spirit moved in His own way. The service went on until midnight. The Lord began to reveal sins and shortcomings to different ones. As they would tell what God had shown them, it would minister to the hearts of the others who were there. Oh, how precious the Lord was to straighten out the confusion in our lives!

Suddenly, one of the men stood in the pulpit. This was unusual. Laymen were not to stand in front. That place was just for pastors and elders. But this brother stood in the front and opened his Bible. I laughed to myself because he had only just repented a few days before this. Oh, this poor brother, I thought. He just repented and now he wants to preach today. He must be crazy.

But he didn't care about how we felt; he just opened his Bible and said, "Brothers and sisters, the Lord told me this is the working of the Holy Spirit." Then he opened to Acts 2, and began to read verse 17: "And it shall come to pass in the last days, saith God, I will pour out of My Spirit upon all flesh: and your sons and your daughters shall prophecy, and your young men shall see visions, and your old men shall dream dreams." After he read all that verse, he began to preach.

After about half an hour, the Lord told him that tomorrow we laymen were to go out and preach the Gospel. That time I just couldn't keep quiet, "Oh, this is unbelievable," I said. "How can laymen go out and preach the Gospel? Why, we've never even been to Bible school or seminary. We've just repented. How can we preach the Gospel? This is impossible." "Brother Mel," this brother answered, "the Lord told me we are supposed to go out and preach the Gospel, and this is the duty of the Christian. This isn't only the duty of the pastors and elders, but every Christian is supposed to stand for Jesus Christ."

I believe now that this is what we have missed in our churches. And I think this is where we have gone wrong. We sit for years trying to figure out everything, completely missing the simplicity of the Word, and so we don't do anything. I thank the Lord that night He began to speak to us and said, "Tomorrow you must go out and preach the Gospel."

In the first three months, we had about 70 groups of laymen that were going out and preaching the Gospel from village to village. And when they went out, great signs followed them, and thus started our Indonesian revival.

At this point I would like to say how amazing it is that through the totally different Revivals, the same convictions still come through. The first is always repentance and the conviction of sin, then comes the urgency to see souls saved. The Great Commission is not just for preachers or those in full-time ministry. This is when forest fires start to blaze and whole communities are changed.

Tari speaks about many miracles happening as the lay people shared the gospel. For example, they needed to cross a river that was over 10 feet deep; they would pray and then ford the river and the water would not go above their knees, allowing them to reach the other side safely.

Tari spoke about food being multiplied: a woman who didn't have much food gave her tapioca roots to the team (just like the Bible story of the hungry prophet, Elijah), and the Lord multiplied it. Tari said there was so much food left over that even the dogs were full – the Lord even took care of the animals.

Even witchcraft had to bow the knee to these Gospel teams; they had witnessed the miracle-working power of the Holy Spirit first-hand. Nothing is impossible for those who believe – it comes back to faith and having faith in God.

As I was waiting to catch a plane to Cape Town, I had a discussion with my television producer and spiritual son, George Carpenter. We were talking about the film clip that had been made of the miracle of En-Gedi. He said that some of his close friends (believers) still doubted the sovereign manifestation by the Holy Spirit. The Bible tells us that even when the disciples were filled with the Holy Spirit on the Day of Pentecost, there were those who mocked them.

> Nothing is impossible for those who believe – it comes back to faith and having faith in God.

Tari talks about whole districts being changed because of the Revival. He mentions children, from the ages of six to ten, who would go to school in the morning and then go home to eat lunch. After lunch these Revival children would meet in groups and they would pray and weep for the lost. Prophetic words would be brought and instruction sought for the specific work God wanted them to do for the lost. On Saturday mornings they would walk through the jungle to nearby villages, sometimes over 8 kilometres away to share the Gospel. Tari asked them if they were afraid to walk through the jungle and they replied, "We have no need to be afraid, for we have an angel in front of us, one behind us, and one on either side of us to keep us safe."

The simplicity of Tari's testimony touched me. Simple, rural people took God's Word literally and applied it to their lives. Sometimes we get too clever and we try to explain and rationalize the commands in the Bible, and then we lose out on the power of God's Holy Word.

I love what Smith Wigglesworth said: "God said it, I believe it, and that settles it." That is why God used Wigglesworth so powerfully – the dead were raised to life, the sick were healed, and his prophetic words came to pass. He walked by faith and fully believed God's Holy Word to the absolute, just like the folk of Indonesia.

Either we take God's Word in its entirety or not at all. We cannot pick and choose. Either the Word is God-inspired, all of it, or none of it. Tari believed that we confess that we believe in the Bible, from Genesis to Revelation.

It happens that if we come to parts of the Bible that tell us something different from what we have experienced, we try to explain it away. I have heard of preachers all over the world who say, "This part of the Bible was not in the original text" or, "This is only for the Jews" or, "This is for another dispensation." We try to figure out the Bible with our minds and in the meantime we lose out on the wonderful experiences of the Bible.

> It is a privilege
> to obey
> the living God.

Many people have not known the reality and power of the Bible in their lives and therefore don't believe the entire book. But the Holy Spirit can help us to understand the Bible as we read it. When I read my Bible I just trust the Lord Jesus. If Jesus says "Jump", I jump – without question. People might think it foolish, but the Bible says that obedience is more important than sacrifice.

People go to church and worship God without being obedient and we need to obey our God. He is a living God and He is working today. I obey because I love Him and because it is a privilege to obey the living God. Did Paul and Silas cry when they were in jail? No, they praised the Lord and, as they praised Him, Heaven came down and shook the whole building. It even shook the heart of the jailer and he said, "Sirs, what must I do to be saved?" (Acts 16:30). The jailer received the Lord that night. When Christians rejoice, heaven comes down and the world rejoices.

In the Old Testament, the Lord told the Israelites to march around Jericho. They obeyed and marched around the city wall and it collapsed. They obeyed the Lord and they won the battle. It is so wonderful to see how God works when we obey Him. It is time that we all obey God, believe His Word and win the battle for ourselves. We need to return to the simplicity of the Bible.

After reading the account of the Indonesian Revival, I felt refreshed by its simplicity. I believe God wants us to stop using our heads and start using our hearts more. Every parable Jesus told was so simple that my small grandchildren can understand them. And yet each parable is totally profound. I think of the parable of the Sower and the Seed, or the Vine and the Vinedresser, the Prodigal Son, and the Good Samaritan. These are such good practical examples of what Jesus wants you and me to do. We need to stop trying to explain the miracles in the Bible and simply believe them – like the island folk of Timor.

One needs more faith to believe in evolution than to believe in the written Word of God. To say that this beautiful universe was created by a "big bang" is nothing short of madness. If we see the intricacies of God's creation, the beautiful fauna and flora, it is amazing. Our heavenly Father was, is, and always will be the Creator of every good and perfect gift. He is the One who sends the mighty winds of Revival.

After my experience at En-Gedi, I am more convinced than ever that our Lord Holy Spirit is alive and well.

There are many things I can't explain although they happened. Jesus said, to one of the wisest men in Israel, that a man needs to be born again in order to inherit eternal life. At En-Gedi I felt as though I was born again, again!

> After my experience at En-Gedi, I am more convinced than ever that our Lord Holy Spirit is alive and well. There are many things I can't explain although they happened.

When Nicodemus asked Jesus how a fully grown man could enter into his mother's womb again, Jesus said, "The wind blows where it wishes, and you hear the sound of it, but cannot tell where it comes from and where it goes. So is everyone who is born of the Spirit" (John 3:8).

I believe, along with four and a half thousand other souls, that that wind at En-Gedi came from God's miraculous power, because we humbly asked Him to do it again.

Saul of Tarsus, who became Paul the apostle, had the "Damascus Road" experience. He had a powerful testimony that spoke for itself – people could either believe him or disbelieve him but they could not argue with him. Felix said of Paul, "You have almost persuaded me to become a believer."

Our experience at En-Gedi is spreading and some people might doubt what took place, but is that any different to what happened during the Upper Room experience? The disciples experienced the baptism of the Holy Spirit, only to be mocked by people down in the street who accused them of being drunk.

I would encourage you to be like those simple peasants of Indonesia, who chose to believe and trust God for the miraculous. They were not disappointed because God visited them. I will never question my God again, when it comes to the fact that He is a miracle worker as well as the weatherman.

FOURTEEN

The Welsh Revival: 1904

The Welsh Revival took place in the early 1900s. God worked through a young coal miner named Evan Roberts. It was one of the most powerful Revivals.

Evan Roberts was a young man who loved the Lord Jesus Christ with an extreme passion and he was used by God in a special way. He had a strong Calvinistic background. He was a sincere man who spent a lot of time in prayer. God used him to shake Wales. Something like two hundred and fifty thousand people were saved and became committed to Christ during this incredible Revival. But it came at a tremendous price for this young Welshman.

Roberts Liardon researched the life of Roberts and documents this in his book *God's Generals*. It is a documented fact that during the first couple of months of the Revival, Roberts slept and ate very little. This rang a warning bell for me. Never ever try to harness a move of God or an awakening. It is too big for a human being to try to direct or manage. We need to understand that we are vessels for God to use. If we try to do the work of the Holy Spirit on our own, it will crush us. That is what happened to Roberts. He tried to direct the mighty rushing wind, something that is humanly impossible. It would be like trying to direct a tornado along a path you want it to go or, harder still, trying to contend with a tsunami – physically it is impossible and spiritually even more so.

Many people were touched by Roberts' incredible ministry. But he did not share his vision; he did not allow the Holy Spirit to lead him or to refresh him or to be his *Parakletos* (Helper) – he tried to do it on his own. Eventually confusion and collapse took place. He suffered a number of nervous breakdowns, and went into isolation. When he came out of isolation he began rebuking people instead of encouraging them. He started to see himself as the Lord's special messenger and the one who was to save the Welsh nation. This was the beginning of his downfall.

> We need to hear from God during times of Revival, because it is only God who will sustain you.

The people who put you on a pedestal are the same people who will knock you off it. We need to hear from God during times of Revival, because it is only God who will sustain you. People will draw from you until there is nothing left, and still draw from you until you collapse.

Roberts started off as a man with a very gentle and loving spirit and yet towards the end, and because of the pressure on him, he started to publicly rebuke Christian leaders and violate his position and calling.

When a person becomes spiritually and physically exhausted, they do not think rationally and become vulnerable to "wolves in sheep's clothing" who give ungodly counsel. These "wolves" start to manipulate and use you for their own ends and this is the beginning of the end. Roberts was eventually looked after by a wealthy lady, Jessie Penn-Lewis. Evan stayed with her and her husband for eight years. He was completely exhausted and, after a huge breakdown, was actually bedridden.

Penn-Lewis tried to help him, and the depressed revivalist was so frail that he succumbed to the teachings of this woman; she was using his name for her own purposes. It went from bad to worse and eventually he began to deny the moves of God that had taken place through his ministry. In essence he said that they had come from the devil. He started to undo every part of the amazing work that God had done through him for the people of Wales.

As I meditated on this man's life, I felt God cautioning me to choose carefully with whom I share intimate things. Jesus said that we should not cast our pearls before swine. They will trample it into the mud and come back and devour you. We need to come alongside men and women we can trust, who will give us good honest advice based solely on God's Holy written Word, the Bible.

Roberts spent eight years with Penn-Lewis and then returned to Wales. He never went into ministry again. He was given a small room to live in by a godly woman, Mrs Williams. She charged him no rent, and she offered him the quiet he needed. He was almost a forgotten man. He spent the last years of his life writing poetry and letters to ministers. He died at the age of seventy-two and was buried in the family plot behind the Moriah Chapel in northern Wales.

This is not intended to discredit the mighty move of God through Evan Roberts, but it is a warning to each of us that no awakening or Revival can be instigated by man – it is by God. God alone is able to direct a Holy Spirit move of this kind. We need to be careful that we don't try to take on the responsibility ourselves.

When God spoke to me at Mhkuze Game Reserve, before the start of the Mighty Men™ Conferences, I had no idea what was going to take place. When the wind of God started to blow, I had a number of respectable men of God visit me and try to convince me to put this move into some kind of "order".

> I know that you can no more box a Revival than contain the wind.

They said we would not see the full benefit of this move if we didn't try to control it! But I know that you can no more box a Revival than contain the wind. What we need to do is acknowledge Who is doing it, do what we can, and leave the rest in God's hands. After all, we are very small cogs in a massive wheel that is being turned from Heaven.

Revival is my subject, it is my passion, and I have made it my life. I have studied most of the Revivals that have taken place and most of the awakenings.

Alexander Dowie was used powerfully by God in the ministry of healing and he became a world renowned figure. He started to build a city, which was to be called "Zion City". He might have done better by building more churches and Bible schools than this huge city. It eventually became his undoing. He was not called to build a city, and instead of doing what he was anointed to do – preaching and praying for the sick – he spent all his time and energy building this city, which wore him out completely.

I believe the same thing happened to Oral Roberts, who built a massive hospital that almost bankrupted him. I do not think that God has raised up many men of the stature and gifting of Roberts. He impacted millions of people with his preaching and healing ministry. The point is that we need to operate in the area and gifting that God has called us to. We shouldn't expand or do something that is not on God's agenda, because it will not have God's blessing on it and will be doomed to fail. The worst of all is that this does not bring glory to the name of Jesus.

Roberts did not rest in God and allow the Lord Holy Spirit to take the responsibility for the Revival. The great

Revival that swept over those beautiful Welsh villages and touched so many souls destroyed him.

Dowie met the same fate. He had been a powerful tool in God's hand. Yet he died at the age of sixty from a huge stroke. He had not fulfilled the total call of God on his life simply because he deviated from the specific task God had given him.

People are influenced more by the way men and women finish the race of life, than the way in which they started it. We need to get our priorities in order and live a balanced life. We need to spend time in solitude with God. We need to fulfil the call Jesus gives us. We need to spend time with our families and keep healthy by living a normal life and taking time out to "smell the roses". If we don't balance our lives we will burn out. That does not bring any glory to God.

> People are influenced more by the way men and women finish the race of life, than the way in which they started.

I remember as a young believer hearing the saying, "Rather burn out for Jesus, than rust out." The truth is that neither of those two bring any glory to the name of the Lord. People are watching us and they are imitating us, even as we imitate the Father, to quote Paul. Often we get caught up in the move of God and we forget to eat and to sleep and to replenish our physical bodies and our spiritual lives. That is why we need men and women of stature around us in times of Revival, who will give us godly input. We need to turn off the phone, close the door, and say, "Sorry, I'm not available." We want to finish the race, and not just finish it, but finish it strong.

I remember an occasion when I was sick in bed (a very rare occurrence) and somebody phoned to speak to me. Jill answered the phone and was trying to tell this man as gently as possible that I wasn't taking calls. My young son Fergus happened to walk into the house at that point and heard this irate man demanding to speak to me, even threatening to take his own life! My son took the phone from his mother and very firmly informed the man that he must do what he must do, but he was not going to speak to his dad!

> It is so important to take time out to spend with your loved ones, to strengthen yourself physically, spiritually, and mentally.

About a year later, that same man drove into the farm to speak to me. Sometimes a person's need is the most important thing in their life at that moment and can lead to unreasonable behaviour. That is why it is so important to take time out to spend with your loved ones, to strengthen yourself physically, spiritually, and mentally.

We need to be still and know that He is God. Jesus did this often; He would go aside to be with His heavenly Father. Sometimes His own disciples would despair because they could not find Him. There would be multitudes of people waiting to hear the Master speak, but He would only come down from the mountain when

His time with His Father was complete, and nothing and no one would take preference over that.

When Jesus did come down to speak to the waiting crowds, it would be to them like manna from heaven, because Jesus had heard from His Father and had spent time in His presence. We need to do the same thing: we need to refresh ourselves, not only in times of Revival, but in life in general. Then we will finish this earthly race strong and not become another sad statistic.

There is no man who can harness the wind – the Holy Spirit blows where He wants, how He wants, when He wants, and for as long as He wants. No organization, no denomination, no group of people can ever claim to have anything to do with the move of God. It is supernatural and never happens in the same place twice (unless God decides to) or in the same way, because God is God, as stated in the book of Job: God is in heaven and we are on earth.

We must never try to presume to tell our God what to do and when to do it; this is a great mistake that many people have made. We cannot capture these "God encounters"; we can only enjoy them, live through them, and be part of them as God allows. Then we thank Him for the wonderful God experience.

I am a completely changed man and will never be the same again. I have realized that I cannot have any control over God's Holy Spirit. I thank Jesus daily for allowing me to have experienced His power and presence in my life. We cannot live constantly on the mountain. Peter, James, and John wanted to do that after meeting with

Jesus on the Mount of Transfiguration. They wanted to build a little booth and stay there with Jesus. But the Lord said no, that the people were down in the valley and that is where they were needed.

We need to spend ourselves for others, but not at the cost of losing our spouse or children. If we lose our families, everything is lost – our testimony, our example, even the divine impact of the Revival. God wants us to grow in the Spirit through these heavenly encounters, so that we can be of greater benefit to others – not to be broken down by it, but strengthened and encouraged.

The Very First Revival

and Our Future

Chapter

FIFTEEN

The First Revival

When the Day of Pentecost had fully come, they were all
with one accord in one place. And suddenly there came a
sound from heaven, as of a rushing mighty wind, and it filled
the whole house where they were sitting.

Acts 2:1–2

The main evidence of the visitation of our Lord
Holy Spirit was the power that the disciples
experienced. The word *power* in the *Oxford
Dictionary* means: the capacity to influence the behaviour
of others, the emotions, or the course of events.

The Lord has affected the course of events in the
world since the Upper Room experience. I have been
to the Upper Room in Jerusalem; I fell prostrate on the
floor and just soaked in the presence of God. It is the one
place in the Old City where there is no commercialism,

no brass hangings or any influence from the past. It is a plain room, but I became so emotional when I thought about this being the place where the very first church met together. The power of God is amazing in that place.

Charles Haddon Spurgeon, a Baptist preacher from the London Tabernacle, said, "There is no telling how much power God can put into a man." Romans 8:11 (KJV) says, "But if the Spirit of Him that raised up Jesus from the dead dwell in you, He that raised up Christ from the dead shall also quicken your mortal bodies by His Spirit that dwelleth in you."

What I love about Jesus is that when He had risen from the dead, through an angel He told Mary Magdalene to go and tell the disciples that He would meet them in Galilee: "Tell His disciples – and Peter – that He is going before you into Galilee." Jesus is so sensitive to you and I, He knows exactly what each one of us is thinking. That is why He is called our personal Saviour. Yes, He is the Saviour of the whole world, but He is my Saviour too.

Jesus knew that the disciples would go down to Galilee to wait for Him, but He also knew that after denying Him three times, Peter probably wouldn't. That is why Jesus sent a personal invitation to Peter and why He asked Peter three times, "Do you love Me?" Peter answered, "Yes, Lord; You know that I love You" (John 21:15–17). Jesus then asks Peter to feed His sheep.

The disciples were told to go back to Jerusalem and wait. Acts 1:8 says, "You shall receive power when the Holy Spirit has come upon you; and you shall be witnesses to Me in Jerusalem, and in all Judea and Samaria, and to the end of the earth." After Peter had been filled with the Holy Spirit, he had so much power that he had no fear of man. Never again did the big fisherman deny the Lord Jesus Christ.

Acts 2:41 says that when Peter went out and preached his first sermon, "Then those who gladly received his word were baptized; and that day about three thousand souls were added to them." This was not the same man who had denied the Lord three times before, so what happened? He received a new language – he could speak in tongues and probably sing in tongues too.

But the main evidence of the baptism of the Holy Spirit was the power that Peter had been given by the Holy Spirit. After the disciples went out from the Upper Room, signs and wonders followed them wherever they went. People would lay the sick in the streets so that when Peter and John walked down the street and their shadows fell on the sick, they would be healed and the captives would be set free. They had the power, they had the gifting, and they had the boldness.

One of my favourite Scriptures is found in Acts 4:13, "Now when they saw the boldness of Peter and John, and perceived [not necessarily the truth] that they were uneducated and untrained men, they marveled. And they realized that they had been with Jesus."

> There was no division, no doubts, no arguments, so the Holy Spirit had perfect liberty to move.

God uses ordinary people to do supernatural works. My only qualification is that Jesus touched my life through the power of the Holy Spirit, nothing else. I have seen Him change the weather, set the captives free, and heal the sick; He is a miracle-working God. He has told us to go out into the entire world and tell people the good news.

Another very important factor that took place in Jerusalem during the time of Pentecost is revealed in Acts 2:5: "There were dwelling in Jerusalem Jews, devout men, from every nation under heaven." Just about every nation was represented at En-Gedi; this was not a coincidence. I believe the Lord Jesus wanted this miraculous manifestation to go right around the world, and that is what happened. A worldwide harvest. I noticed an important ingredient in that meeting, and it was unity. There was such love and acceptance among the different nations.

Our Father reminds us that where there is unity, He commands a blessing (see Psalm 133). There was no division, no doubts, no arguments, so the Holy Spirit had perfect liberty to move and to flow wherever He desired. It was the ideal setting for a visit from the Holy Spirit.

We cannot demand or try to coerce the Holy Spirit to visit a meeting or conference. The disciples were visited when the Spirit of God said the time was right. He goes when He sees fit because He is God.

I believe that the greatest Revival that this world has ever seen is near to breaking out. We, as the bride of

Christ, need to be prepared and ready. So put aside any doubt, scepticism, and judgment and allow the Holy Spirit to take full control of every aspect of your life. He will direct your paths all the way Home so you have nothing to fear.

Job 19:25 says, "For I know that my Redeemer lives, and He shall stand at last on the earth." Jesus will come back. He is alive and He is with us in the presence and person of the Holy Spirit.

Don't harden your heart towards Him. As we know from Hebrews 13:5, He is a Friend, someone who will never leave us and never forsake us.

References

Chapter 11
Olea Nel. 2008. *South Africa's Forgotten Revival*. Xulon Press. USA.

Chapter 12
Duncan Campbell. 1956. *The Price and Power of Revival.* Public domain.

Chapter 14
Mel Tari. 1971. *Like a Mighty Wind*. New Leaf Press.

Chapter 15
Roberts Liardon. 2003. *God's Generals*: *Why They Succeeded and Why Some Fail.* Whitaker House, PA.